holding
hope

One Family's Odyssey

through Lyme Disease and Psychosis

MARABAI ROSE

BEAVER'S POND
PRESS

ISBN 13: 978-1-64343-674-6
Library of Congress Catalog Number: 2022918788
Printed in the United States of America
First Printing: 2022
26 25 24 23 22   5 4 3 2 1

Book design and typesetting by Dan Pitts.

Beaver's Pond Press
939 Seventh Street West
Saint Paul, MN 55102
(952) 829-8818
www.BeaversPondPress.com

Contact Marabai Rose at marabairose.com for speaking engagements,
book club discussions, and interviews.

To Milo and Annika

You inspired me to find strength when I was feeling weak, to look for the light when I found myself in darkness, and to rejoice in a boundless love I had not known before. For the both of you, I am forever grateful.

November 8, 2014
5:15 p.m.

The stretcher holding my body is moving quickly down a hallway. I catch flashes of doorframes, men and women in scrubs hurrying past, the fluorescent lights so bright the darkness is streaked with a neon green when I close my eyes.

"Are you having any trouble getting a breath?" asks the respiratory therapist, keeping perfect time with the stretcher as it speeds toward its destination. I can see her eyes watching my chest. She has been silently counting the seconds between each inhale and exhale.

"No," I mutter through the oxygen mask. My voice is thin, too quiet. Fifteen minutes earlier my arms went dead, and I cannot lift the mask to make myself intelligible.

The RN running alongside the stretcher looks at my face closely, quizzically, and asks, "Marabai, is it getting harder to breathe?"

My breath feels no weaker than it did ten minutes ago, the last time I had to breathe into a tube so they could measure my breath's ability to sustain my life. I manage a louder and more decisive, "No."

I wonder what they are seeing, but I don't have enough breath to ask.

I glance from face to face and see the anxiety etched into the firm shape of their lips.

I am hurtling toward a room where I will receive a CT scan to make sure my brain is not bleeding.

My terror rises when I hear the respiratory therapist say the scan has to be done quickly because she thinks I am moving into respiratory arrest.

My breath stays with me until I am back in the first room with my husband, and the machines, and the doctors and nurses surrounding me, and then it is nearly gone. Just a brief flutter at the top of my lungs. I understand now that I will stop breathing. I can't speak. I look into my husband's eyes and he understands too. Suddenly everyone in the room understands.

I want them to understand so they can help, yet my body rebels when I hear the doctor declare it's time to intubate.

I imagine a breathing tube forced down my throat.

My throat closes reflexively, but I won't fight the intubation because I want to live.

The faces of my children come into my mind, clear and radiant, and I want to live.

My children need me.

My husband needs me.

There is not enough air in my lungs to speak this truth, so I declare it silently to myself. I want to live.

Part 1

Chapter 1

In August 2014, I was thirty-seven years old. I was a wife, a mother, and a social worker. My assessment of my own life at this moment was largely positive. At thirty-four, I'd undertaken a mission to improve my health after I had my second child and found myself chronically exhausted. I gave up sweets and became one of those obnoxious people who tells you the secret to life is to practice yoga. My energy levels were high, and my stress levels were low. I felt great. I reduced my hours at work to give myself one day off per week to use for self-care. My nine-year-old son and four-year-old daughter were thriving, and I was in love with my husband of eleven years, Scott.

Scott and I had our challenges. He had a Jekyll-and-Hyde quality that I was able to recognize as a mood disorder; however, he was not able to name this, or accept it. The tension around his mood was the undercurrent of our lives. He would have long periods of depression, and bouts of irritability that left him hyper-critical. He was also controlling. I attributed this to his anxiety. I imagined he needed to closely manage the details of our lives because his anxiety often made him feel as if things were spinning out of control.

I asked him to go to individual therapy numerous times; he refused. We tried couples counseling, but he would not admit to experiencing depression or mood swings in front of our therapist. Trying to talk to him about it myself was futile—any mention of words like *depression* would set him off. He would tell me I wasn't allowed to label him. He would turn the focus to me, telling me if I treated him differently, if I kept the house better, he wouldn't feel this way. It was jarring. Just as I began to consider leaving him, he pivoted, becoming loving, kind, generous, a 50/50 partner to me in caring for our home and our children.

Scott's bond with our kids was incredible, and his tenderness for them drew me closer to him. In good months I tried to forget about the times he would suddenly fill with anger, picking at the slightest thing I, or one of the kids, had done. These outbursts were incredibly unsettling because they were at odds with the gentle version of him that was often present.

I didn't know what to do. I loved him, and he loved me. He seemed to understand on some level that his behavior was hard on me, because when he had the capacity to be caring, he worked very hard at showing up for me. So, it became an unspoken agreement between us—I would ride out the bad times with him, and when he was in a good space, he would give me the things he couldn't when the darkness overtook him. Somehow, at age thirty-seven, this balance appeared good to me. I would have told you, had you asked, that we had a good marriage. At least on the surface. I quieted my intuitive voice enough to successfully shove aside the misgivings I had about my husband.

My career path had placed me at an inpatient hospice in a mid-size, midwestern college town. My pull to hospice social work began with my first job out of grad school. I worked as a crisis mental health counselor in flooded areas of my home state. It was a great way to sharpen the most important skill a social worker has, the ability to build relationships quickly. Knocking on the doors of flood survivors' homes, I had about thirty seconds to earn their trust. I had to have that receptivity to do my job, to be invited into their lives, to hear their stories.

In moments of grace, I might be able to find words to hold them, to validate them, and plant a seed of hope. I heard many, many stories over the course of eighteen months. Tales of the mayhem the flooding had caused, but also descriptions of deaths, divorces, children lost to drug addiction, relationships lost to conflict. It was an incredibly intimate experience, sitting with these humans and their grief. It reaffirmed my decision to become a social worker. Before long I realized sitting with loss seemed to come naturally to me, and I felt called to be a hospice social worker. I was hired to be a medical social worker for home health and hospice in 2010, and I settled into the work.

Health care was woven into my family line. Four of my five immediate family members had worked for the same hospital that housed my hospice department. My mom, an RN, had walked the units of this hospital for decades and spent time in the technically challenging and heart-wrenching area of critical care. She gained a great deal of experience tending to patients at the end of life. She was skilled at having the very hardest conversations, asking families to consider quality as opposed to quantity of life. My mom wound up working in the same hospice as me and we got to share our professional experiences with each other. My brother Ben and my father worked at this hospital for years in different roles. This hospital was a place I strongly associated with family. Every time I walked through those doors someone who knew my family would approach me and ask about them, and me, and my kids. I felt so much warmth and caring in those hallways.

Being a hospice social worker gives one a unique perspective. You watch people face death over and over. You watch families become intimately aware of what their dying loved one truly means to them. You glean wisdom from dying patients who pull you in close to tell you *"What really matters are the people in your life."* You come to value health, as you watch people struggle with illness. You feel deep gratitude for your good fortune.

I loved interacting with my patients and their families, and while I was not thrilled by working for a large health-care system, the rewards outweighed the hassles. Up to this point, I did not consider myself overly taxed by my job.

However, that August, I began to have a quiet, nagging feeling that something wasn't right. I felt exhausted at the end of each day. I told myself hospice work might be more draining than I realized, and I should ramp up self-care. I scheduled a week off in October to use as retreat time; a time to practice yoga and recenter myself. I talked about my feelings with my mentor Pat, who was supervising me as I worked toward becoming a licensed clinical social worker (LCSW). After Pat and I talked for a while, I concluded this fatigue was due to changes at work. Our small hospital had merged with a corporate health conglomerate, which had caused a great deal of upheaval for myself and my coworkers. I thought things would settle into place eventually.

One evening toward the end of the month, I attended a school fund-raiser at Western Skateland with my son. Never one to care if I looked goofy, I strapped on skates and awkwardly rolled around the rink with him, relishing the fact that he would still allow this. I stood chatting with another mom, Lisa, when I suddenly lost my balance and went down. I instinctively put my hands out to catch myself and hit the ground hard enough to break the scaphoid bone in my right hand. Looking back now, I can see this chat with Lisa was the last moment I would have as a healthy person for years to come.

The bone's healing was slow, and I found myself tired and overwhelmed. Everything at work suddenly seemed impossible, and I barely had the energy to cook a meal for my family, which had always been something I loved to do. I chalked it up to my hand being broken and can remember having conversations with friends about how much energy healing bones takes. When the cast, and then the brace, were finally off, though, I still did not feel my energy return and went back to believing I just needed a week off.

On October 28, 2014, I turned thirty-eight. I chose to take my vacation during that week of my birthday. I decided to use the time as a yoga retreat, but instead of traveling to a fancy destination, I would stay home and take classes at my own yoga studio to save money. On October 27, my first day off, I was disappointed to find I was coming down with a cold. I went to yoga that day and the next, but after a birthday lunch with a good friend, I decided I had to lay low because I was feeling sick and spent. I worsened over the next five days at home, surprising myself, because I typically bounced back quickly from the common cold.

On Monday, November 3, I called in sick to work and noticed throughout the day that I was having trouble catching my breath. The congestion from the cold had cleared up, so my shortness of breath seemed odd. I was overwhelmingly fatigued, and now every time I walked to the bathroom I was panting. I had never experienced anything like it and made an appointment to see my family doctor the next day, November 4.

By the time of the appointment, I was dramatically short of breath and so winded walking from my car to the door of my doctor's office, I could barely get inside. My doctor gave me an inhaler to use and ordered a chest X-ray. Back at home that evening, I didn't notice the inhaler making much of a difference. I was still panting from minimal activity and tried to stay in bed as much as possible. My doctor called me the next day to give me the results of the chest X-ray, which were normal, and assured me my symptoms were due to a virus. She told me not to worry.

The following day I still wasn't feeling any better, but I allowed my daughter to stay home with me instead of going to preschool. I thought we could snuggle and watch movies together. By 10:00 a.m. it became clear my cozy day was not to be, as I sat in my kitchen barely able to breathe. I dialed my doctor's office. She said I could be hyperventilating, but I should go to the ER just in case. Because I had never suffered from an anxiety disorder, I felt it was more likely physiological in origin and called my husband to come get me.

In case I was hyperventilating, I found a paper bag and began breathing into it, like I had seen in movies. When Scott arrived I was a mess, barely able to get a breath in, tears streaming down my face. He loaded our daughter and me into his truck and sped through town, glancing at me constantly to make sure I was still breathing. The crinkle of the paper bag and my ragged breath were the only sounds in the car.

In the emergency department I was given immediate attention. A nebulizer treatment, where one inhales steam made from liquid steroids, was first used to get my breathing under control. When the nebulizer failed I was given an injection of steroids, which worked temporarily, but then my breathing began to get ragged again, and another nebulizer treatment was given.

I was diagnosed with adult reactive airway disorder and sent home with steroids in pill form, along with muscle relaxers to help the muscles of my chest wall loosen up.

Despite following all the instructions I had been given, the very next day I was back to being short of breath. All day long, without relief, I struggled. My husband was extremely worried and called a doctor we knew personally to get me some other kind of help. An at-home nebulizer machine was ordered and I began inhaling steroids every four hours.

My days began to revolve around the nebulizer treatments. I would immediately become short of breath as soon as I was up and moving around the house. I would use the nebulizer, get relief for two to three hours, and then spend the one to two hours before my next treatment short of breath. I was bone tired, weak, and pale, and the nebulizer treatments made my heart race and my hands shake. My husband, self-employed as a carpenter, quit going to job sites and stayed by my side, helping me to the bathroom and bringing me food. I kept catching him watching me, a worried expression on his face. I looked terrible, and we both knew it. Yet we hoped the virus theory was correct, each of us wanting to believe I was having a few bad days but would get better. I worried about having to call in sick all week when I had taken the previous week off, but there was no choice. I couldn't walk to the bathroom on my own, so I certainly couldn't work. There was nothing to do but watch and wait.

With each passing day, I became more debilitated. Within three days of my first doctor's visit, my legs became profoundly weak. I noticed they felt heavy, as if my muscles weighed three times more than usual. I couldn't lift my back leg off the floor to meet my front when I took a step, so instead I dragged it forward, foot scraping the ground. Then, as I was walking upstairs to lie down in my bed, my legs gave out entirely. I was able to lean on the wall and slide down, landing softly on my bottom at the foot of the stairs. I was not injured, but I could not get back up. I called for my husband to help me to the couch. He called my doctor insisting there was something really wrong. She and I spoke on the phone, and her assessment was that I had a very severe virus and was experiencing muscle weakness due to it. I remember for the first time hearing my own intuitive voice saying, *No, something more serious is going on.*

Unfortunately, what came out of my mouth was, "I am scared." I later learned admitting fear to a doctor will instantly invalidate your symptoms. Although I can't say with certainty what a doctor thinks when they hear a patient's fear, my guess is they assume the fear is inflating the patient's description of their symptoms; the fear is creating symptoms through anxiety; the fear is distorting the reality of their experience, transforming the patient into an unreliable historian. Of course, when your most basic abilities, like walking and breathing, are under attack, you will be afraid. Terribly afraid. My fear was met with reassurances that were not reassuring, because I knew something was attacking my body, and I did not know what it was or where help existed. I was too listless to argue, so I just accepted the reality of being sick and on my own. I didn't know what else to do.

On November 8, a Saturday, I awoke to discover my legs had not recovered from the night before. I could not walk on my own, and my poor husband had to practically carry me to the bathroom. When I caught a glimpse of myself in the mirror I was shocked to see that my skin and lips were the pale gray I had observed on my extremely ill patients in hospice. I had become too exhausted to think or make decisions.

Scott seemed to understand this, and instead of asking me if I wanted to call the doctor again, he just did it. He described my condition and asked to bring me in. The person he spoke to stated the office was closed and they couldn't see me until the following week, but she would talk with my doctor about his concerns. I watched my husband's face stiffen with frustration, the muscles in his shoulders tensing. When he hung up a pang of wanting my mom hit me. I wished for her loving presence, her medical knowledge, her help with the kids. However, she'd had surgery on her foot the day before and was in no shape to leave her house. The kids drifted in and out of my peripheral vision all morning as I lay on the futon, too ill to explain what was happening. I hoped someone was taking care of them.

My husband was upset and felt like he needed a break from the worry, so he asked my brother Sam to come and sit with me and help with the kids. Sam arrived by midday. My best friend Hannah also came over to check on me. When she greeted me, I could see fear move into her eyes as she scanned my gray face, took in my panting breaths. She asked what was being done to help me, who we were communicating with? Someone, I don't remember who, reassured her, explaining that we had another call in to the doctor and were awaiting a response. My best friend and brother took their spots next to the couch to wait with me, while Scott took our dog Clyde out for a hike.

Around 2:00 that afternoon, while Scott was still out, my doctor called and told me she had been researching my symptoms and it was possible I had an autoimmune disorder. She said it could be serious and I should go to the hospital. Hannah wanted to take me right away. Yet, I hesitated. Scott knew the whole story up to this point—the ER trip, the doctor visit, the phone calls—and I knew I couldn't communicate all of that with my faltering breath and crushing fatigue. There was something else too: Scott's presence was comforting. The thought of going to the hospital without him, facing testing and possibly a scary diagnosis, was unacceptable to me. So we waited.

Like everything else in this moment, Scott's hike went sideways. Clyde ran away and would not return. Scott had to look for the dog for an hour before returning home, and by the time he arrived there was a sense of urgency pulsing through our small living room. As soon as Scott walked in the door Sam and Hannah went into action, explaining to Scott that he needed to take me to the hospital—now. My husband was clearly overwhelmed; he questioned if I did need to go, and what exactly was happening.

I can remember the exasperation on Scott's face as he said he had to make himself a cup of tea and gather some things. I was lying there watching the figures of my family float around me; it was as if my voice had vanished. Everything felt slow and heavy—my movements, my thoughts, my intentions. Buried underneath the lethargy was a sense my time was running out, so when my husband was finally ready to take me to the hospital, I was relieved. Sam would stay with the kids and await news from Scott. Hannah was living in a city an hour to the north at the time and had a five-month-old daughter, who was currently being cared for by her mom at a friend's house in our town. She needed to get her daughter and go back to her home but asked Sam to keep her in the loop when Scott was able to tell them what was happening.

Loading me into the car was no small feat as my legs were not functioning at all. My brother and husband had to carry me, an arm slung around each of their shoulders, legs dragging behind. After lowering me into the front passenger seat, they had to lift my legs and place them in a forward position for me, as I was too weak to manage it.

I realized, in addition to my leg muscles going limp, the muscles in my torso seemed to be melting against the seat as I leaned against it. My head slumped forward. Seeing my slack posture seemed to be what my husband needed to grasp the sense of urgency Sam and Hannah had exhibited, and he quickly entered the driver's seat and began to speed down our road. We made progress until we hit the first major intersection on our route just as a college football game was letting out. Our town is home to one of the largest universities in the Midwest. Football traffic is no joke. The moment we were swallowed into traffic I tried to lift my hand to brush my hair out of my face, and I realized that I couldn't.

Looking ahead at the long line of traffic, I said to my husband, "Scott, I just lost my arms." I still had control of my neck and turned my head to see him, to gauge his reaction. I could see panic flicker across his face, but he stayed calm. He found a way to make a U-turn into another lane that was not as outrageously congested, but still we sat and sat. Finally, my husband leapt out of the car and ran ahead, stopping at each car in front of us and explaining the situation. Because this is a town of nice Midwesterners, every single car in front of us pulled over as far as they could and let us through.

Thank God they did, because within the next hour I would stop breathing.

I was grateful to see the red glowing letters spelling *Emergency Department* as we pulled into the covered drop-off zone. My husband was able to get immediate attention and I was quickly triaged and brought back into a treatment room. Within minutes of being hoisted onto the bed and having my vital signs taken, one of my best friends, Annie, walked into my room in her red RN uniform. Annie was working as an ER nurse, and when she saw my name go up on the board she hurried to my room. Just as Hannah's expression had communicated concern when she first saw me, Annie's face flashed with fear. Just as quickly she put on a smile and walked up to me with a list of calmly worded questions.

In these moments I remember the overwhelming sensation of anxiety as my body became gradually less and less under my own control, but also a profound feeling of safety: I'd made it to the hospital, and here was my friend to make sure I was taken care of. Also, my respiratory therapist just happened to be a childhood babysitter. This space, the ER room, was familiar as I had visited patients from home health and hospice who had ended up here. I had sat with victims of rape in these rooms as an on-scene advocate. I had a sense, whatever this was, that the solution was close at hand, and I would be okay soon.

I could not have been more wrong.

The next hour was a blur of tests; a stream of nurses, doctors, and respiratory therapists in and out of the room. The same questions asked over and over: What were my first symptoms? How long had I been experiencing profound weakness? When was I first short of breath? As my own ability to speak and think waned, my husband took over answering these questions. At some point, after it was determined I was likely experiencing a neurological event, the on-call neurologist arrived on the scene. While everything had felt on fast-forward before, the quick determined movements of the staff, the rush down the hallways to get to the CT scan, and the arrival of the neurologist seemed to move us into warp speed. I was so far gone, I couldn't concentrate on what the nurses were telling me. My body was impossibly still amidst the blur of activity in my peripheral vision. All I knew in those moments was that I was going to stop breathing at some point, and I desperately needed someone to do something about it because I wanted to live.

I was diagnosed with Guillain-Barré syndrome, and the neurologist explained to me that what was happening to my body was destructive, fast acting, and possibly permanent. Guillain-Barré is a disorder in which your immune system goes rogue. It is triggered by a virus, and instead of your immune system attacking the virus, the immune system attacks the myelin sheath on your nerves, damaging them and causing paralysis of the limbs and, in some cases, the muscles that control your breathing. In acute cases of Guillain-Barré, patients must be placed on a ventilator to breathe for them due to the diaphragm's inability to activate the lungs. Mechanical ventilation, often referred to as *the vent* or *life support*, requires being intubated. Intubation is a procedure in which a breathing tube is inserted into a patient's throat, where it sits at the top of the lungs forcing air into them. It is a powerful tool in the arsenal of Western medicine, allowing patients to live when they are too weak to breathe for themselves.

The neurologist realized it was time to intubate when my muscles stopped responding to the stimulation that usually causes reflexive movement, and the latest respiratory assessment showed another decline in my lungs' ability to move air. I was relieved, as I could feel the lack of motion in the lower parts of my lungs each time I took a breath. That sensation had been slowly moving up my chest, until my breath was reduced to a slight movement at the top of my chest, barely perceptible.

I was frightened by the idea of intubation, yet more frightened by my chest's stillness. No one asked for my consent to intubate me. I wouldn't have been able to speak or nod if they had. My whole being was still now. The only thing moving in my body was my fear, threading through my heart, widening my eyes. I hated the idea of a hard tube penetrating my throat, *But what choice is there?* I asked myself. I knew the answer was none; there was no choice but to stay alive, by whatever means necessary.

Chapter 2

After my flaccid body was wrapped in a bedsheet and lifted by many hands onto a stretcher, I was wheeled to a cold metal table in a sterile operating room. I didn't shiver when my skin made contact with the metal—my muscles were beyond that. Instead, I felt the cold seeping in, going deeper into my tissue until it hit bone. The light above my upturned face was blinding. The neurologist who had treated me in the emergency department was suddenly at my side, briefly leaning over me to check my pupils and make sure I was still breathing; this time he was wearing the gauzy apron and cap of a surgeon. I couldn't turn my head to look at him as he stepped back and spoke. His voice seemed to be coming from the edge of the white orb that filled my vision. He explained that before inserting the breathing tube he needed to perform a spinal tap, so that laboratory testing could confirm the diagnosis of Guillain-Barré. One of the indicators for Guillain-Barré is elevated cerebrospinal fluid protein.

There were hands on me again, rolling my body into a side-lying position, gently pushing my knees up toward my chest. I was facing away from the doctors as they began to swab my back with a sharp-smelling fluid. The needle used for the procedure was a size that makes you think, *You have got to be kidding me* when you see it. Unfortunately, I had caught a glimpse of it, laid out on a metal tray, as I was being hoisted onto the table. The anesthesiologist was on hand to administer a local anesthetic, and then the neurologist pushed the huge needle into a space between my vertebrae, looking for the sac that held my spinal fluid—and he missed. He had to repeat the procedure with the help of the anesthesiologist, and in the process created a small tear in my fluid sac, later resulting in the worst headache I've ever experienced. Having spent several minutes barely breathing by this point, the panic I initially felt had transformed into a hazy, disconnected feeling. It was as if I were moving farther away from the metal table with that strange still body on it with each passing second. When I was successfully tapped, the hands reappeared, rolling me onto my back. Finally, they gave me the anesthesia that allowed me to drift away and inserted a tube that would push oxygen into my lungs for the next three days.

The following hours of total darkness were the most peaceful I would experience for months to come. They were not, however, so peaceful for my husband, who was watching my intubation through a glass rectangle in the metal door leading to the operating room. I can't imagine what it was like for Scott that day—the helplessness of watching me fade away, losing movement, speech, and color. He could see my fear, all the way to the intubation, and there was nothing he could do to take it from me. The fear was something we shared, and those dark, quiet hours of sleep gave me some respite that he wasn't privy to.

Immediately after the intubation the neurologist told Scott the Guillain-Barré syndrome was acute to the point where I was a candidate for all of the worst outcomes. They didn't believe I would die, because death in Guillain-Barré usually results from someone losing respiratory function prior to getting into a hospital setting and then dying of respiratory failure. The doctor did believe it was possible I would never walk again, though, and never regain full use of my arms. I could end up wheelchair bound and require a great deal of assistance to get through my days. If I did walk, the doctor explained to my husband, it would be after a long, intensive rehabilitation period that would likely last a year or more.

At the time my husband was hearing this information, our children were four and nine years old. Imagine working through the reality of caring for an adult woman, a four-year-old, and a nine-year-old, while also solely responsible for supporting them financially. Scott later told me this moment, when he heard that I may never walk again, was the worst of the whole ordeal for him. Not only because of the burden it represented, but because Scott loved me. He loved me fiercely. His awareness that my body and way of life were suddenly being taken from me, and imagining my grief and devastation, was too much to handle. My husband would carry it with him, these moments, this stress. The weight of it would crush him over time.

After the intubation I was moved to the critical care unit. My husband sat with me the entire night in a chair that would become my family's post for days. I don't know if he spoke to me, or if he sat in silence. I do know he held my hand, stroked my face. While I have no memory of his touch, I know this to be true because it was how we were with each other. When Scott's depression and anger weren't twisting him up and robbing us of connection, we anchored each other with touch. We were always reaching for each other, pulling each other in. Kissing in the kitchen, leaning against one another as we collapsed, exhausted by work and parenting, into our nightly ritual of binge-watching *Mad Men* or *Breaking Bad*.

I can picture him sitting in my hospital room with the eerie glow filtering in from the fluorescent lights in the hallway, the green and blue coming off the monitors filling the space between us. I can imagine his overwhelm, powerlessness, as he watched the machine breathe for me. I hope some small part of him could rally and whisper to his pessimistic spirit, *It will be all right*. It had always been my job to insert optimism into his worldview, but my voice was quieted, buried underneath medication, a disease process, and a breathing machine that would save me and torment me all at the same time.

There are many ways in which doctors attempt to make time on the vent bearable for patients, mostly by completely knocking them out so they sleep through the entire experience. I wasn't so lucky. In my case, they needed me to be awake so they could check for voluntary movement. Therefore, a medication called midazolam (more commonly known as Versed) was administered. Versed will prevent a person from creating new memories while on a high-enough dose, so they won't recall the hard tube down their throat when the time comes (hopefully) to remove it. This is referred to as a *conscious amnesia*.

The Versed did not rob me of my memory; instead the medication fragmented it. I can't be sure if my first memories are from when I was summoned to consciousness by the lessening of the more powerful anesthesia that kept me under, or the first time my mind broke free of the Versed-induced amnesia and began to create them. I do remember the awakening. It began with a twilight sleep, my brain just coming to terms with the world around me existing again after a deep slumber. I fully expected to be in my own bed at home, pulled into consciousness by the jostling of my four-year-old crawling into bed for good morning snuggles at an obscenely early hour. As I tried to turn over and peel back the covers for her, as I had on countless mornings, two things occurred to me in rapid succession:

1. *I couldn't move.*
2. *I had something in my throat.*

My eyes sprang open in fear and surprise. I was in a room full of machines, my mom and husband by my bedside in armchairs upholstered in a bad imitation of blue leather. Immediately I tried to speak, to ask them how I got there, and what was going on? As my mouth attempted to form words the air from the breathing machine pushed the sound back into me. My throat constricted with the effort of speech, creating the first huge burst of pain as my inflamed throat tissue made contact with the tube. Immediately, the sensation of the back of my throat touching hard plastic caused my gag reflex to go into overdrive and my throat engaged in a succession of spasms, each more painful than the last. I remember my mom coming close, placing her hands on my forehead, telling me to try to relax, try to stop swallowing. Her touch was so calming I could do as she asked.

The two days after were like living in a dream state from which I would occasionally awaken. Most of my conscious memories from this time hold fear and pain. I recall the panic in my chest when my own mucus temporarily clogged the breathing tube, suffocating me for a short period. Yet the sensation of the suction device scraping my tender throat was no better due to the searing pain it caused. This was a ritual that would repeat itself every few hours.

I remember waking early one morning; it was one of the rare times there was no family with me. I had been given paper and a pen to write messages, and I remember writing to the nurse, asking her to call my husband. I needed him next to me. I was so scared and it was his touch I wanted. When Scott arrived he moved his chair as close to the bed as he could get, and he held my hand. I was still awake, and we held each other's gaze. He told me how much he loved me while tears spilled from the corners of his eyes. He spoke of the pain the thought of losing me had caused, and the regret as well. He acknowledged how he had not always seen my value, but in this crisis he did. I could feel the intensity of his love pierce me, and I was psychically shouting back to him, *I love you too! I was scared of losing you too.* I think he heard me, because in that moment of my unspoken affirmation there was something that united us. For the next eleven months we would be a team, committed to fixing my broken body.

In the ICU, everything is measured: your temperature, urine output, blood pressure, oxygen saturation. Blood cells are counted, reflexes are tested. By all those accounts I was not well. My legs were described as *flaccidly paralyzed, with no deep tendon reflexes,* meaning I had no ability for voluntary movement. My diaphragm was measured each day and in the first forty-eight hours found to be too weak to support breathing independently of the machine. A feeding tube was inserted through my nostril and into my stomach to nourish me.

The physicians treating me thought an infection had set off this whole cascade of events. My blood work indicated some sort of infection, but they were unable to identify it. I was diagnosed with pneumonia based on the respiratory symptoms I had presented with in the emergency department the week prior, despite that I wasn't diagnosed with pneumonia at that time. They needed to have an infection to fight and pneumonia made the most sense. I was given a strong IV antibiotic, Cefepime, as it would cover many of the possible bacterial invaders. The treatment for Guillain-Barré syndrome is intravenous immunoglobulin therapy, more commonly referred to as IVIG. It introduces antibodies into your system to fight infection, and in the case of Guillain-Barré, to stop the rogue antibodies from attacking your nerves by flooding them with healthy antibodies. IVIG is typically given for five days consecutively when used to treat Guillain-Barré. As soon as I was stabilized and placed on the vent, IVIG was started.

My brother Ben, a physician, drove from Wisconsin to be with me. Ben was granted a seat at the table with the doctors treating me, as he had been an oncologist himself in this same hospital and had a collegial relationship with the men in charge of my care. It was a difficult spot to be in, brother and doctor. He told me there were times when he would be hearing the medical details of my case, as he had so many others, and then be struck with the thought, *This is my sister we're talking about.* His presence was invaluable, both to my recovery, as I had a motivated doctor in my corner with a direct line to those in charge, and as a conduit of information for the rest of my family.

My mom, a skilled and intelligent nurse, often played the role of medical translator when someone in her life had a medical event. However, my illness had undone her. Seeing her daughter on a ventilator. Seeing her daughter with lifeless limbs. Seeing her daughter lying in the same room where she had attended to patients, some of whom had died. It was visceral. She was also just days out from her own major surgery, and in great pain. Mom was not able to be the medical interpreter, so Ben stepped into the role.

By the end of day three I regained voluntary movement, my reflexes becoming intermittent at first, then consistently present. For someone with complete paralysis from Guillain-Barré this was a highly unusual outcome and my family was overjoyed. I was also becoming more and more agitated by the vent. The respiratory function test (known as a negative inspiratory force or NIF) given the morning of my third day in the ICU showed I was just below the level of functioning where I could breathe on my own again.

By that evening I could not bear another minute on the vent. It was the torment of suction that did me in. With my arms working again, I had begun to suction myself, so I could control where the suction tool landed in my throat. My saliva and mucus were blocking the vent tube yet again, and it was taking a bit longer than usual to clear. The entire time the tube is blocked it feels as if you are suffocating, and my panic and frustration were rising with each second. Because I had to clear the mucus out, I allowed the suction tool to graze the back of my throat causing a moment of eye-watering, all-consuming pain. As soon as I cleared the vent, I picked up a piece of paper and wrote to the nurse in attendance, "Get this tube out of me or knock me out. Now." I couldn't take being awake on it any longer. The doctors needed me awake to assess my level of weakness, so there was a good rationale for everything they were doing, but I couldn't be a trooper anymore.

The nurse offered me the pain medication that had been ordered, but I refused. I continued to write demanding messages to the nurse and to Ben, who was keeping watch at my bedside. With his professional sway, Ben was able to call the pulmonologist back. I was later told the pulmonologist was a bit grumpy about this and hesitant to even attempt extubating me. My brother convinced him to order another NIF and if I passed, I would be taken off the vent.

This NIF is the only one I remember out of my time in the ICU. I can clearly recall when the air from the vent stopped pushing itself into my lungs. I could feel my lungs rejoice in the freedom to create their own rhythm as I pushed the last bit of canned air out forcefully so the respiratory therapist would see I could do it, and took in a giant inhale. I remember how irritating it was when they immediately turned the ventilator back on until they could run everything by the doctor, but the look on my brother's face told me I had passed the NIF with flying colors.

Quickly the decision was made to pull the breathing tube. The final indignity of having the tube yanked out of my throat, gagging me and drawing mucus into my mouth, was made worthwhile by the liberation of breath. I was also freed from the feeding tube. It had to come out when the breathing tube did, and it was pulled through my nose, creating some sensations I hope to never experience again. While all of this was thoroughly unpleasant, it was also deeply restorative. My body was becoming my own again. I felt an internal shift, beginning with the writing of the note. I felt powerful as I took in some hard-won breaths, moving through a sore, but independent, throat.

I would spend three more days in the ICU, finishing out my course of IVIG and antibiotics, and having my strength assessed each day. There was always another milestone to look to. The first time I got out of bed, my legs were too weak to hold my weight. I was simply transferred to a chair. I began to weep as I sat in that chair, every muscle in my body trembling with effort; it was clear I was a shell of the woman I had been only a few weeks before. I remember saying to the physical therapist helping me, "I used to be strong." However, in a turn of events surprising the medical team and my family, I rapidly recovered from what we thought was Guillain-Barré. Within just a few days I was walking the hallways with a walker and another person always close at hand. I was sitting independently for longer periods of time, and all of my reflexes were perfect.

The grim picture painted by the neurologist in the ER had not come to pass. It seemed I would fully recover, and quickly—much more quickly than the majority of Guillain-Barré patients.

I had overcome many of the hurdles by day six of my hospitalization but had one major lingering issue. I had an insane headache, unlike any I had ever experienced. My nurses talked to the doctors over my days in the ICU, and my pain medication was continually upgraded until I was on fentanyl for the pain, but it still wasn't enough. Finally, it occurred to the medical team that a tear in the spinal fluid sac might be causing the excruciating headaches. A young anesthesiologist was called in to do a "patch," where an injected fluid closes the tear and fixes the problem. Just a few hours after the patch the headache had completely vanished and I was without pain for the first time in days.

In numerous ways I seemed to be a best-case-scenario patient. All of the worst possible outcomes predicted at the outset gave way to the best possible outcomes. I was walking independently, and there was no lasting impact on my arms. I was tired from all I had been through but could tell my strength was beginning to return. My family rejoiced as it became clear I would make a full recovery. I was told I could expect to be back to work in a month if I continued to improve at this pace. It was as if a miracle had occurred, and I was being handed my life back. My physician brother shared his theory on my quick recovery, positing that getting treatment as quickly as I did helped negate the long-term damage. Whatever the reason, it seemed as if I had beaten the odds. I was jubilant.

One of the truly astounding things about this time was the outpouring of support from my community. My sister-in-law immediately began a Go Fund Me site and hundreds of people donated to support my family so my husband could be by my side without worrying about the bills. My dear friend Amy, a powerhouse of compassionate energy, created a meal train for me. When I mentioned I hated the hospital food, she had the meal train start immediately and I was brought home-cooked food in the hospital. She came to me and told me there were more people who wanted to bring me meals than there were meal slots to fill, so I asked her if people would want to bring coffee and breakfast since the hospital coffee was dreadful. Many friends got up early and brought me delicious coffee and breakfast items for the rest of my days in the hospital.

I received hundreds of messages of support on my Facebook page, and by the time I moved to rehab I had enough cards to cover the face of my closet door, taped in place by my family who wanted to remind me I was loved. I remember feeling a bit bewildered by the depth and breadth of the support, but deeply grateful. It is something I will never forget. It is a great blessing to know the compassionate side of the human heart, to know what nurturing and grace we are capable of.

Chapter 3

I was transferred to the acute rehab unit in the same local hospital after a short stay in progressive care, and the trajectory maintained its positive bent. I flew through my physical and occupational therapy sessions in the first week, quickly getting to the top of the scoring chart. In the second week, though, I began to notice that while I performed well in the sessions, the impact of the exertion was changing for the worse. I needed to lie down between each session, and my arms and legs would feel heavy. My physical and occupational therapists seemed to think this was normal given everything I had been through, and I was encouraged not to worry. It seemed the staff was genuinely happy for me. They explained many times over that most of their Guillain-Barré patients were markedly debilitated by the disease, and here I was effortlessly balancing on one leg or climbing stairs. Their enthusiasm was contagious, and I pushed the disquiet of those heavy limbs aside.

Less than two weeks after being admitted to acute rehab I was given a discharge date. Prior to discharge, patients did one community outing with an occupational therapist to make sure they could navigate the world with their new set of limitations. I was excited to get out of the hospital and had chosen to go to a large grocery store, Kroger, where I did my weekly shopping. My mom would accompany me on this outing and drive me there, where we would be met by my occupational therapist.

When the day arrived, I felt strong on the walk to the car. Strong when

I walked through the parking lot into the store. My mom and I quickly located Laura, my occupational therapist. The three of us began to weave our way through Kroger in a little cluster, with me in front pushing the cart, and them trailing by a couple of feet, watching me intently. I am not sure what the other Kroger shoppers made of our little group. It must have looked like I was being stalked, or followed by spies who were very bad at being inconspicuous. After pushing the cart through a few aisles, I still felt my legs solidly under me, my muscles working normally. I felt giddy with relief. *I can do this,* I thought. *I really am okay.*

In the pasta aisle something began to shift. Suddenly, I felt dizzy and strange, as if the voices of the people standing next to me were ten feet away. I then felt a tremble go through my body; the kind of tremble your muscles experience after an intense workout. I must have said something, although I can't remember what. Laura seemed to understand I was at risk of going down right there. We were in a very large Kroger with a Starbucks and a lounge area. We moved quickly toward the lounge area where I could sit and recover. I held tight to the cart for support as we raced through the produce section and past the green and white of the Starbucks stand. We made it to a worn, dark-blue love seat where I collapsed. I rested my head back against the cushion, allowing the love seat to take all my weight. I noticed my legs were quiet, the trembling suddenly replaced by a feeling of vacancy. It was familiar. This same feeling stole over me amid my first episode of paralysis.

I was thunderstruck by fear while desperately trying to move my feet, realizing they were gone. A numb feeling was crawling up my body, the same way it had weeks before, and I felt dread like ice in my veins. There was no vent here, no doctors. "What if I stop breathing?" I asked Laura.

"Then we will call 911," came her matter-of-fact reply. She stayed calm.

I couldn't stop asking the question, "What if I stop breathing?"

My mom was ashen with worry and holding my hand, which she could feel going cold. Laura seemed to understand the words I needed to hear, saying things like, "Your breathing is fine. If it becomes labored, we will call for an ambulance, but right now it is fine." The cold numbness had spread into my arms at this point and I was unable to so much as wiggle a finger. Then it crept up my neck, causing my head to loll at a weird angle on the dingy love seat, where countless others had sat sipping their lattes and taking a break from shopping.

The last to go was my face.

The muscles went slack. I couldn't speak. I couldn't move my eyes. I stared vacantly at the ceiling screaming a silent prayer, "Please don't let me stop breathing, please don't let me stop breathing." My tear ducts still worked. I couldn't blink, and a stream of tears began trailing the sides of my face, pouring from my wide-open eyes as I lay there.

I was splayed on the love seat, limbs askew and entirely motionless for what felt like hours but was actually just a few minutes. Finally, a tingling sensation crept into my hands, a slight warmth returned, and I wiggled my fingers. More tears fell in response to my relief. My body was coming back online before my diaphragm quit.

I picked my head up and looked down at my still quiet legs. I was in disbelief that my body had collapsed on me again. Laura and my mom both began to relax when it was clear I was going to be okay. As soon as I could use my legs again, we left the grocery store, all of us anxious to get back to the hospital.

After returning to my hospital room a wave of homesickness washed over me. I felt certain this episode meant more time there, more tests, more nights trying to fall asleep in a tight, hard bed.

I missed my family. I wanted this to be over.

Unbelievably, the new onset of temporary paralysis did nothing to slow down the discharge process. I happened to be a patient in the acute rehab unit as one doctor was leaving his position and another was taking over. I have wondered if I may have gotten lost in the transition, because the new doctor began working with me the day after the grocery store episode and didn't seem to know about the incident. My sense was he didn't really want to know as I tried to bring it up.

My discharge date was set for two days after I had become paralyzed again. I was so ready to be home I did not object, even though the episode of paralysis was deeply troubling. No one attempted to explain why it had happened, and in the vacuum of information I assumed that it was a normal part of recovering from Guillain-Barré. So, finally, on a chilly November Wednesday, I was able to return home after sixteen days in the hospital.

Although I was genuinely happy about the idea of being reunited with my family, I was a little nervous about how Scott would handle the stress of caring for me as I recovered while also being the primary breadwinner.

Within the past year we had gone through a rough patch where Scott hadn't worked for four months due to a deep and prolonged depression. This depressive episode drained the life out of him; he retreated to the couch where he would lay and read all day. He stopped working without discussing it with me; in fact, he barely talked to me. I would try everything to engage him, and repeatedly asked him to get help, but I realized it would just be a matter of waiting it out. During this time I was afraid I wouldn't be able to support us all by myself, and I remembered that fear, how it felt. Now I knew with certainty that I wouldn't be able to support our family, at least not for another month or so. I silently prayed for Scott's capacity to grow enough to meet this new set of circumstances.

Scott had prepared a space for me on our downstairs futon, purchasing a memory foam topper and new pillows to help make me comfortable. The house was suddenly filled with adaptive equipment. When I was leaving the hospital the occupational and physical therapy staff had helped me pick out items I could never have imagined needing a month earlier: a wheelchair, a shower bench, handrails for the bathroom. It seemed unnecessary to me at the time, but they were insistent. As part of my discharge my insurance would cover it. If I ordered these things later, it might not.

In just a few short weeks I would come to rely heavily on all those items.

At first, being home was perfect. I slept better in my own bed than I had at the hospital. Being able to sit at the dinner table with my family felt good. My daughter stayed close to me in those early days. She had always been a child who needed proximity to her mom. When she was a toddler I had to create a spot for her right next to me, no matter what I was doing. After spending more time apart than we ever had in her lifetime, she created a little world on and around my futon in the living room, her Playmobil princesses and dress-up clothes littering the floor around the legs of the futon. There were piles of books within arm's reach we could read while lying down together.

My son was the opposite. He looked at me warily, like he wasn't sure if it was safe to approach me. After a couple of days, he began to quietly sit on the edge of the futon after Scott took our daughter up to bed. He wanted to play with the smartphone Scott had purchased for me when I was in the hospital. Quickly he found comfort under the sleeping bag which was always on my body. We would curl up together, taking pictures of ourselves in an app that allowed you to distort your image as if you were in front of a fun-house mirror. We would laugh together at clips from *America's Funniest Home Videos* circulating on YouTube. I enjoyed the sound of his laughter, the warmth of his not-so-little body. Slowly, he seemed to accept this new mode of family existence.

My experience of happiness was short lived, as I quickly found myself deeply fatigued. At the hospital I was up out of the bed for hours each day. Within a week of living at home, I found myself struggling to be up for more than fifteen minutes at a time. Soon, just walking to the bathroom was enough to cause me to have to lie down for an hour or two.

My mom was there constantly, and her face betrayed deep concern as I rapidly regressed. My husband was growing worried as well. Me? I was drifting into a place of being too tired to worry. Fatigue can zap you of the mental and physical energy to do anything outside of basic existence. It was as if I were underwater, watching the world around me blur and become more distant the deeper I sank into the fatigue.

On my fourth day home I had another episode of paralysis. Much like the one at the grocery store, it started with a dizzy, faraway feeling and progressed quickly, moving up my legs, my arms, my torso, and finally to my face. The face was the most disturbing aspect. It was frightening to not be able to communicate during these episodes. It must have been horrifying for my loved ones to see my face go slack, all expression and personality washed away. It is what our faces do in death.

The question on everyone's mind was, would I stop breathing again? We were all aware that if my diaphragm muscles had quit on me before getting to the hospital on November 8, I could have lost my life. This fear hung over us like a fog.

We had an appointment with an outpatient neurologist for three weeks after my discharge. Our first move, after getting through the shock of the episode of paralysis at home, was to call him. I fully expected to be told to go back to the hospital, or at least that I would be seen in the office the following day. It was quite the opposite. It took two days for the office to even return our calls. When the receptionist called back, Scott was sitting by my side. Her voice was loud enough that I could hear her, and her irritated tone, from a few feet away. She informed Scott that the doctor would not see us prior to my scheduled appointment. When my husband explained the concerning possibility I would stop breathing in the midst of one of these episodes, the receptionist told him if I stopped breathing he should call 911.

Imagine sitting with that possibility. Your wife may stop breathing and you may have to keep her alive until the ambulance, which would be fifteen to twenty minutes away, arrives. It seemed impossible this was the response from the doctor.

The episodes of paralysis began happening more frequently until they were a daily occurrence. They were accompanied by a host of strange sensations in my body. An intense buzzing would sometimes pop up in my left ankle, keeping me awake at night. My fingertips and thumbs would at times feel as if they were on fire, like they were being seared, especially when I touched cold water.

No matter how carefully I planned my activities, I couldn't keep my energy level consistent. I plummeted after doing anything: sitting for a meal, taking a shower. My mom began to bathe me while I sat on a shower chair, like I was a little girl again, because the effort of lifting my arms to wash myself would wipe me out for half a day. Upon discharge I had been told I could expect to have my energy level gradually improve and it would be no problem to return to work in January. Yet two weeks after arriving home I found myself totally debilitated and with no explanation as to why. We were counting down the days until our neurology appointment, hoping this doctor could explain what on earth was happening to my body. In the rare periods of mental focus available to me I began researching Guillain-Barré.

My assumption all along was this experience of regressing into profound weakness must happen to people recovering from this syndrome. What I found was quite the opposite. No tale of Guillain-Barré I read about sounded quite like mine. The beginnings were definitely similar: ascending paralysis after a viral or bacterial infection, intubation, then rehab. However, this is where the experiences diverged. In the literature, those with acute Guillain-Barré, where mechanical ventilation was required, spent six to twelve months in acute rehab relearning how to walk, use their arms, and sit unassisted. Many would go on to have permanent weakness in their arms or legs. I found no mention of an acute Guillain-Barré patient seeming to make a full recovery, and then regressing.

I found no evidence of the neuropathies, those strange sensations that plagued me, and definitely no descriptions of intermittent paralysis. My experience up to this point had been frightening, but it had a name; the disease followed a path; I could look ahead and see where I was going. Now I was lost. Suddenly nothing made sense. I began to question the diagnosis.

When the day finally arrived to see the neurologist, we were desperate for answers. The episodes of intermittent paralysis were now happening most days, and my husband and I had both reached the conclusion this did not make sense for Guillain-Barré. The neurologist immediately agreed with our conclusion. He stated it seemed very unlikely I actually had Guillain-Barré syndrome, and he wanted to run a huge battery of tests to see what was going on. Neither the doctor, nor I, faulted the physicians at the hospital for diagnosing me with Guillain-Barré. The onset was identical to Guillain-Barré, with ascending paralysis and respiratory decline, following a virus. It made sense, and I knew that the care I received that day had saved my life.

I trusted this new doctor's assessment. It felt aligned with what I had been reading about. It was reassuring that he affirmed the conclusion I had come to, that the typical recovery from Guillain-Barré differed greatly from my experience. This doctor appeared to be a caring person, who took me seriously. I was soothed; he seemed to be looking into all possible causes and appeared certain we would find the answer. I left the appointment feeling more hopeful than I had in weeks. Our follow-up appointment was a month away, however. The doctor explained he had to send some of the blood samples to the Mayo Clinic lab for specialized testing. It would take time to get all the results back. A month seemed an impossibly long time to wait, given how seriously ill I was. I had no choice but to stick it out, though, hoping I could weather whatever my body threw at me.

In the ensuing weeks I deteriorated. The most basic functions of life—eating, bathing, walking to the bathroom—became heroic feats of strength. If I could have had a catheter, I would have welcomed it. There were numerous times when I ended up on my kitchen floor while trying to walk back from the bathroom, arms and legs splayed and lifeless as my body shut down from the effort of those fifty steps. The living room became the place I lived. My family spent all their time with me there until I became too tired to talk, and then my husband would redirect the kids to other activities. My color began to change again, back to the cold gray it was when my illness had first become severe.

Again, we reached out to the outpatient neurologist numerous times, questioning if I should be in the hospital, asking what this decline meant, begging for an earlier appointment. His office staff was always curt, seemingly affronted by how my precipitous decline was of such concern to us. Finally, in desperation, after a week of daily episodes of paralysis and weakness that had me bound to my bed except for the necessary trips to the bathroom, my husband drove me up to a hospital an hour away in our state's capital city. This hospital was supposed to have the best neurologists in the state, and we were determined to get an answer to the riddle of my declining health.

I was quickly admitted through the emergency department. It took most of the day for the hospital to secure a room on the neuro unit, and by the time they did, it was late evening. My husband was exhausted and felt he couldn't stay in the hospital with me. My mom was taking care of the kids, and with me in the hospital he could get his first real break in weeks. He drove home and I was left by myself. It was frightening to be suddenly alone in a strange hospital in a different city, but I was so bogged down by the fatigue I couldn't really interact with the fear. It was just there. Sitting on my chest. There when I went to sleep. There when I awoke.

The hospital did put a lot of eyes on me; I was paid visits from numerous doctors. I had an internist, a neurologist, and even a pulmonologist because of the respiratory issues during the last hospitalization. I was monitored constantly, and many more tests were done.

When I posted on Facebook to let my community know I was back in the hospital, a friend wrote to me saying my illness sounded like ehrlichiosis, a tick-borne illness. I asked to be tested for ehrlichiosis and Lyme disease. They gave me the first step in Lyme testing, the ELISA (enzyme-linked immunoassay), to look for the presence of antibodies to borrelia, the bacteria that causes Lyme disease. If the ELISA finds antibodies to borrelia, then the patient will receive a test called a Western blot. The ELISA was negative. I was not given a test for ehrlichiosis. The doctors did nothing more to look at tick-borne illnesses.

An electroencephalogram (EEG) was ordered to test my brain activity. The EEG required hospital staff to glue electrodes to my scalp to measure the electrical activity in my brain. My hair was covered in glue, and I looked like a mechanical Medusa. A magnetic resonance imaging test (MRI) was ordered and took hours to perform. I was placed in a narrow, claustrophobic tube where bizarre noises ricocheted around me as magnetic and radio waves worked together to create detailed images of my spine and brain.

After three days of testing and examination the neurologist finally had a possible explanation.

It was New Year's Eve, and he came to my room while my brother Sam and best friend Hannah, who both lived in the city I was hospitalized in, had come to visit. When I saw the neurologist walk in looking determined I was flooded with relief. *He will finally tell me what is wrong with me*, I thought. *I will have a plan to get better.*

After asking if I wanted my visitors to stay (I did) he launched into a long explanation about how the testing had all come back normal—they couldn't find anything wrong with me and he thought I might have had Guillain-Barré in November, but now, his best guess was that I had a conversion disorder, a psychiatric illness. He was careful to say he didn't know for sure, but it was a possibility and he thought I should consult with the hospital's psychiatrist.

He asked me if I knew what a conversion disorder was. I said, "Yes" and thought, *Better than most of your patients do.* You see, I had a master's degree in social work with a concentration in mental health and addiction. I had probably spent more time with the *Diagnostic and Statistical Manual of Mental Disorders* than this doctor had. It was as if the floor opened up and I was falling. A conversion disorder?

For this to be true, my brain would be creating physical symptoms as a way to cope with my stressors. Conversion disorder affects people who have experienced a traumatic event and have not discovered a way to effectively deal with the trauma, so their mental suffering is expressed in physical symptoms.

I began to run the diagnosis through my mind, thinking about the wide variety of symptoms I had experienced: fatigue, neuropathies, the extreme muscle weakness caused by any type of exertion. It just didn't add up. Yes, the experience of being on a ventilator was traumatic, but I was sick before then. Prior to being placed on the ventilator I had no significant trauma history, and I was managing my stress well with my reduced hours at work and my yoga practice. The diagnosis of Guillain-Barré had quit making sense when my recovery after receiving IVIG and IV antibiotics was too quick given the acuity of the initial onset. I was left with the question, *What had made me so sick in the first place?*

I felt certain there was something attacking my body from within. I was sick, way sicker than when I had been discharged from the hospital. I voiced my concerns, and the neurologist didn't press the point any further but did reiterate I should meet with the psychiatrist. I agreed to it, because I figured the psychiatrist would see it didn't add up. No history of trauma and an overarching illness made the diagnosis feel like total nonsense to me.

Because it was New Year's Eve, I was told that the psychiatrist would not be able to meet with me until January 2, and my frustration began to boil over. I was not going to sit in this hospital for two days just to have this dubious diagnosis checked out. I asked to go home and the hospital was happy to oblige. I called Scott to ask him to come get me and was discharged quickly. Arriving home, I was more bewildered and disheartened than ever. While I didn't believe the doctor's diagnosis, my confidence was shaken. I began to question my reality. *Am I somehow fabricating all this?* I had already lost control of my body, and now the health of my mind was called into question. It was a difficult thought. Even so, my optimism hadn't been entirely quashed and I held out hope for the outpatient neurologist visit taking place approximately a week after leaving the hospital.

I was certain the outpatient neurologist would find the diagnosis laughable. There would be some other solution offered, and I wouldn't be left to languish in this illness any longer. The day came and my mom took me to the appointment. I remember how fidgety I felt. The normal heaviness of my limbs gave way to my legs kicking the air as they dangled off the table, the nervous energy coursing through me. The neurologist came in and with his kind bedside manner, asked me if I knew what I had been diagnosed with at the larger hospital. "A conversion disorder," I said, "but I don't think the diagnosis is right."

The neurologist looked at me with great empathy and began to explain that the entire thing, the first paralysis, the vent, the rehab, was all part of a conversion disorder.

There was actually nothing wrong with me.

I began to sputter my dispute. "I didn't have reflexes—how can a conversion disorder take away your reflexes?" and "I was placed on a vent; they tested my breathing and it was failing. How would my breathing fail from a conversion disorder?"

Again and again, he shooed away my questions, giving me vague answers and stating he hadn't seen that detail in my chart (although I checked later, and it was all there). He maintained the physicians treating me had made a mistake in placing me on the vent. "They overreacted," he said multiple times. When I brought up the fact I had no history of trauma, no major losses, no abuse or neglect in my past, he actually told me I had probably been sexually abused as a child and blocked it out. He said this in front of my mother. He told me his office would set up a psychiatrist appointment for me and there was nothing more he, or any other medical doctor, could do for me.

I was, in essence, ushered into the wilderness with this diagnosis. With a conversion disorder on my chart, no doctor would take my condition seriously.

When he left the room, I lost my composure and found myself wracked by sobs. The fear, pain, and hopelessness had been building since the first episode of paralysis in the grocery store. I couldn't contain it any longer. I wasn't going to get help. I was on my own with this thing, and it was ruining my life. There was nothing I could do and no one who would help. I cried the entire ride home. I sat in my bathroom and cried for another hour, hiding myself away so I didn't scare my children who had just arrived home from school. Scott sat with me in the bathroom holding me while I cried, staying silent, because what was there to say? There was no clear path forward, and we were both terrified and helpless in the face of this nameless illness. Not only was I left without a diagnosis and treatment path, but I was also to blame for being sick in the first place. If these doctors were to be believed, I was sick because I hadn't acknowledged and dealt with my stress. Even while largely rejecting this diagnosis, there was a part of me that took it on. A part of me felt incredibly guilty for putting my family through this hell. A part of me felt as if both my body and mind had betrayed me. I was utterly lost.

Chapter 4

I continued to intermittently lose all function as I entered 2015, making it necessary for someone to be with me at all times. Leaving the house required the use of a wheelchair and came with the risk of public paralysis. I needed a grab bar to get off the toilet and, much to my embarrassment, sometimes a physical assist. Most of my days were spent in bed, ashen and lethargic. Scott had to go back to work so one of us was earning money, and we were both overwhelmed.

All throughout January and February my dear friend Amy organized volunteers to sit with me for forty hours per week so Scott could work. We were concerned over the possibility I would stop breathing due to the intermittent paralysis; a person with me at all times made sense. Having been a hospice social worker I had seen many people in the same situation, needing care due to weakness, and I knew what a challenge it could be. Here I was with a stream of people in and out each week, volunteering their time to sit with me. Being an extravert, I credit those fine humans who made their way out to my little bungalow as a major reason I did not become clinically depressed. There were so many kind faces to brighten my day.

On top of the physical care I was receiving, the meals kept coming. My friend Mandi, who owned a cleaning company, brought a team to clean my house top to bottom at no charge. I was getting so much support from my community, at times I found myself crying with gratitude, so overcome by this love.

I held a deep conviction that the diagnosis of conversion disorder was wrong and went to my primary care physician (PCP) with hope for an answer, feeling fragile from my last two experiences with doctors. I was asking for help in figuring out what could be ravaging my body. I was a thirty-eight-year-old woman, who two months prior could hike ten miles, do intensive ninety-minute ashtanga yoga classes, and work a demanding job while raising two kids. Something had happened to cause total paralysis, leaving me in a state of debility, unable to leave my house except for essential reasons like medical appointments. The only thing the physicians I saw during that time seemed to agree on is I did not have Guillain-Barré syndrome. All the weird and varied symptoms were still there—the buzzing sensations, the recurring paralysis, the muscle weakness after the mildest exertion.

I saw my PCP in her office. She and I talked through all that had happened since November 8. It was now mid-January. I was at two months of illness and counting, and no one seemed to have any idea why I was still so sick. Sadly, my family doctor was just as stumped and gently trying to get me on board with the conversion disorder diagnosis because she didn't know what else it could be. She told me the emergency room physician who had treated me in November had called her just after I was admitted to the hospital to report what had happened in the ER. She mentioned the ER doctor said I had been anxious. I felt frustration bubble up inside of me as I thought, *Who wouldn't be anxious about becoming fully paralyzed and requiring intubation?*

It was thoroughly demoralizing to have her support the idea of conversion disorder, as she knew me and the whole story of my illness better than any of the other doctors involved. I pushed back, telling her I was certain the diagnosis was wrong. My PCP told me the only other thing it could be was chronic fatigue syndrome. Chronic fatigue has no known cure, and I was told I might just have to learn to live with the limitations. I couldn't conceive of living with this illness long-term. I was a shell of the woman I once had been. I couldn't take care of my family. I couldn't work. I shuffled out of the doctor's office feeling desperately sad.

At home with the kids present, Scott and I would retreat to the bathroom when we needed to talk. Shortly after my family doctor diagnosed me with chronic fatigue we were in our usual posts, me on the high-backed chair sitting across from the tub, he perched on the toilet lid. We were discussing what route to take next and who I could see, but we kept coming up against the barrier the conversion disorder diagnosis had created. Scott's expression pivoted from sad and confused to fierce as he said, "It's sexist."

As soon as he said it, I felt it deep in my gut, a naming of something that had been pulling at my mind for weeks. Yes. It was sexist, and as I would find out, I was having an all-too-common experience for women with a rare medical condition.

Conversion disorder is rooted in the Freudian concept of hysteria. Freud believed women were converting their psychological issues into physical symptoms. When modern researchers have examined historical hysteria cases, many of the symptoms explained by Freud and his colleagues as hysteria could be attributed to medical diagnoses not yet discovered, such as syphilis and epilepsy. The diagnosis of hysteria continues to exist but is now known as conversion disorder. Today, women are diagnosed with conversion disorder up to ten times more frequently than men. Per an article in the *AMA Journal of Ethics*, "Recognizing and Treating Conversion Disorder," studies show 25 to 50 percent of individuals diagnosed with a conversion disorder are later found to have a medical condition that could cause the same symptoms bringing them in for assessment. In addition to conversion disorder, women's medical conditions are also commonly misdiagnosed as anxiety and depression.

In some cases, the consequences of this widespread sexism are fatal. Women have a 50 percent higher chance of getting an incorrect diagnosis after having a heart attack. Women under fifty are more than twice as likely than men to die from cardiac arrest in a hospital setting. A study titled "The Girl Who Cried Pain" found women were less likely to receive appropriate treatment for pain and more likely to be dismissed as "emotional," or to have their symptoms considered psychogenic ("It's all in your head").

After Scott and I talked, I realized I would never have any answers until I submitted to a psych eval. I had to have the conversion disorder diagnosis debunked before anyone in the medical establishment would take on the task of figuring out what was really going on. I allowed my PCP to make a referral to a local psychiatrist. This psychiatrist wanted the psychologist in her office to evaluate me. It took four weeks to get my first appointment, and she could only see me once every two weeks. I would need to see her three to four times for her to agree or disagree with the diagnosis, meaning I would have to wait months before being cleared for further medical testing. Months of disabling physical symptoms, not being able to work, not being able to parent my children, not being able to support my husband. I thought to myself, *If I wasn't crazy already, this process might drive me there.*

My time with the psychologist was not all bad. She was friendly, and it was nice to have someone to talk with about my grief over losing my life as I knew it. I expressed my confusion and fear around what this illness was and why it couldn't be named, my frustrations with the medical world that branded me as mentally ill when they couldn't come up with a better diagnosis.

In the meantime, it was dawning on me that I had better take matters into my own hands. I wasn't being given any options for healing from the Western medical world, so I would need to ramp up research and begin to heal myself in whatever ways were available to me.

I began to search the internet for herbal and alternative options for recovering from a neurological illness—this was my best guess as to what afflicted me. I began to make changes on my own. I gave up coffee, which was impressive as coffee had been one of my great loves for many years. I saw a physical therapist who was also an energy worker, and I benefited from his holistic approach. I began acupuncture with a practitioner of Chinese medicine who was an extraordinary healer. She had been practicing acupuncture for decades. She was the first practitioner who not only took my situation seriously, but gave me a path forward. Presciently, she told me she knew I would recover, but it would take two years.

She began treating me with weekly acupuncture sessions, placing needles all across the plane of my body. In her large, cluttered office, with Chinese illustrations of the nervous system on the wall, she told me she sensed my brain and nerves weren't communicating well, and therefore she wanted to stimulate the nerves throughout my body to be more receptive to my brain's signals. It was almost comical how unpredictable she was in terms of how long I would lie there with needles all over. Sometimes it would be an hour, sometimes three hours. She used her intuition each time to know when to take out the needles. I would lie there praying I wouldn't need to pee before she came back. It would be unwise to get dressed with hundreds of needles sticking out of you, or to waddle to the bathroom naked, looking like a porcupine.

Within weeks of starting acupuncture, the intermittent paralysis began to dissipate. At first the episodes began to space themselves out, going from daily, to every three days, to one time a week. I could now tolerate being out of bed for short periods. By February I began to putter around my house for thirty-minute stretches of time. Given my confinement to the futon for two and a half months, those thirty minutes felt like sweet freedom. Scott had been carrying the entire load of the housework and the childcare for months, and he had been gracious about it. I was happy to be able to pitch in a little. Finally, toward the beginning of March the episodes of total paralysis stopped altogether. I still experienced significant weakness in my limbs after any exertion, but I retained more control of my body. I also added in reiki, massage therapy, and supplements like vitamins B and D3 to help with my energy level.

Still, the limits this illness placed on my life were real, and while I was grateful to be improving at all, the state of my body terrified me. I was still so affected by something I had no name for. There was an ever-shifting aspect to the symptoms. I would have a better day and think I could do a normal task, such as picking up my daughter at preschool, only to have my legs give out on me during the short walk down the hallway to her classroom. A version of this story happened at the grocery store and in medical offices, my legs and sometimes my arms quitting on me, leaving me stranded, splayed out in some hallway, waiting for someone to come by so I could explain my situation and get some help.

At the beginning of April my psychologist told me she was ready to make an official recommendation for treatment. She said she did not see enough evidence to support a diagnosis of conversion disorder and would write a letter to my PCP advising I get sent for further medical evaluation. While I was relieved and vindicated, I also realized the next step was not clear. I had already seen several neurologists, none of whom were able to give me any helpful answers. I was beginning to fear there was no help for me out there. I was all alone in this illness. This feeling made seeking assistance again seem very high stakes. I felt vulnerable turning myself over to another unknown doctor. What if they had no answers either? What would I do?

My PCP wanted me to see a rheumatologist and made a referral, only for us to find out the one rheumatologist in town was booking appointments six months out. In some ways it felt like being back to square one. I was angry. Disputing the conversion disorder diagnosis had robbed me of months where I could have been looking for answers. I felt unclear where to turn next. I needed to get a diagnosis and start treatment for this illness that had turned my life upside down for nearly five months now. While I should have been happy to have my intuitive voice validated, instead a sense of hopelessness crept in.

My son turned ten on March 30. I was too sick to attend his birthday party at a local bowling alley. It was the first birthday I had missed. My mom offered to make his birthday cake. I had always made my children a homemade cake on their special day. Whatever they wanted, no matter how complicated, I would make it. I couldn't make my son's cake, and the disappointment I felt was unbearable. I held it together until Scott and the kids were packed up and gone, and then I cried bitterly, tethered to the futon again. There were many parenting moments I had lost already in the previous months. I couldn't hold my daughter's little body as she fell asleep because I couldn't climb the stairs to her bedroom. I couldn't take my ten-year-old out for hikes to the creek near our house, looking for crawdads and geodes together, his little scientist's mind delighting me.

Throughout the week my energy level improved a bit, and on April 6, when my daughter's fifth birthday rolled around, I decided I was going to make her cupcakes. The mixing and baking part of the process was smooth, but by the time the frosting began I was exhausted. My mom, who was often on hand to fill in for me, told me I was too tired and needed to lie down. But I just couldn't give the job of frosting the cupcakes over. It was the most important part. So I sat slumped at the table, trying with all the strength I could muster to pick up the frosting with a knife, spread a layer on the cupcake, and then use my decorating tools to make something beautiful.

Except I couldn't. My arms were too weak, and my hands lost their grip; instead of frosting cupcakes I sat in a state of abject despair. I couldn't do this one thing I so wanted to do for my daughter. It didn't matter to me if it got done anyway, I didn't do it, and it was *my* job. After five months of debilitating illness a voice crept inside of my head. It whispered in my ear, *This is your life now. It will never be any better than this.* Sitting dejected at the table with my useless arms, frustration boiling inside me, I felt betrayed by my body. That voice sang its siren song, *You will never make a birthday cake again.*

Chapter 5

Repeatedly losing control of my body was terrifying and not something I can muster much gratitude for in the "lessons learned/silver linings" type of reflection I am sometimes capable of. However, I am grateful for just one of the scary medical events that took place in the spring of 2015. The event brought me into contact with the very first medical provider to suggest I may have a tick-borne illness.

In all fairness, an acquaintance had made this suggestion multiple times, as early as December of 2014. But she was one of dozens of people who reached out to tell me they thought they knew what was wrong with me, or what I should do to get better. From diets to diagnoses, I received so much unsolicited advice. It is an undeniable human impulse to solve problems. The problem of my mysterious illness was intriguing for many, and I did not have the capacity to seriously entertain all the theories. In part that's because considering any diagnosis involved a moment of hope in which I'd think, *Maybe this could be the answer*, quickly followed by the crushing realization that the symptoms didn't match up. My own research dragged me through this process again and again. So to engage with others in their medical sleuthing just felt like too much.

In early May I was at home with my husband. We were sitting across from each other at the kitchen table, talking about the mundane functions of our homelife, when suddenly I went stock still, arms dropping to my side. I found myself frozen. I couldn't move my face, my eyes fixed to the map of the world across from me, above Scott's head. Scott began repeating, "Marabai, Marabai, what is going on?"

I couldn't respond, I couldn't look at him. My right arm began to tremble, then launched into a full, spastic tremor, shaking the right side of my body while my left side remained perfectly still. I remember crying from fear and having the tears only exit the right tear duct. It was bizarre. Another new facet of this waking nightmare. While we were both dubious about the medical system at that point, we were also totally freaked out and needed to know we had done everything to figure out what was going on.

We arrived at the ER that evening wary, expecting a whole new slew of tests revealing nothing. With the pain of the conversion disorder diagnosis still fresh, I fully expected to be dismissed as crazy. Happily, it was not my fate. After the usual checking in and waiting for several hours, a woman who looked to be in her mid-thirties entered the room and introduced herself as a physician's assistant. A physician's assistant (PA) has the same power to assess, diagnose, and treat a patient, but does so as part of a medical team including a physician who can oversee the PA's work. The PA sat down, made eye contact with me, and truly listened as I explained what the previous six months had held. She told me, given the fact that I had a normal EEG just five months before, she did not think I was having seizures, but it seemed like I was experiencing symptoms from a yet-to-be-diagnosed medical condition. She then asked me if I had been tested for Lyme disease. I told her I had, but since learned the testing could be unreliable (this was told to me by the acquaintance who, thankfully, was one of the more persistent medical sleuths in my community). She encouraged me to find a practitioner who was knowledgeable about tick-borne illness and explore the idea further. She was kind, respectful, and not dismissive in the slightest. I cried with relief as Scott guided me through the ER hallway in a hospital wheelchair back to our car.

That night, after putting our children to bed and helping me to bed, my husband sat on the computer and searched. He searched half the night, until finally he found what we had been looking for all these months: the Columbia University Irving Medical Center's Lyme and Tick-Borne Diseases Research Center. The center's website detailed the symptoms of each known tick-borne illness circulating in the US today.

On the website Scott found two illnesses, ehrlichiosis and anaplasmosis, that cause both adult respiratory disorders and have central nervous system manifestations, including symptoms that mimic seizures and neuropathies. Thinking back to what he had seen me experience, he was putting it all together. I had a week of severe respiratory distress followed by months of symptoms related to the central nervous system (paralysis, tremors, seizure-like events), along with a host of strange bodily sensations such as burning skin, buzzing ankles (i.e., neuropathies). My symptoms matched perfectly with the tick-borne illness symptoms listed on the website. It was, at last, our eureka moment.

When I awoke in the morning, he told me with absolute conviction he had found it, and as soon as I read through the symptom list I knew in my bones, indeed, he had.

I immediately scheduled an appointment with my PCP for the same week. Not only did the Columbia University website describe my illness, but it also offered treatment recommendations. Finally, I was within reach of a solution and all I could focus on was the freedom treatment offered. I also contacted my local network of friends and family asking if anyone knew of a practitioner who was comfortable with tick-borne illness. I was given the name of a local nurse practitioner in private practice who was just beginning to treat tick-borne illness.

I prepared for my appointment with my primary care physician as if I were preparing for a major presentation at a board meeting. I printed all the materials supporting the diagnosis and made a list of all my symptoms from the previous six months to cross-reference with the symptoms listed in the literature. I knew the exact name and dosage of the medication recommended to treat this bacterial infection. I was not going to be dismissed. Not this time. I enlisted one of my fiercest friends to attend the appointment with me, so if my arguments fell on deaf ears I would have backup. In reality, my PCP was very caring and supportive, yet I had felt so discouraged by our last visit, my defenses were up.

The visit went as well as it possibly could. My PCP was able to see enough similarities between my symptoms and the symptoms listed on the Columbia site, that she felt comfortable prescribing the recommended medication, doxycycline. She also seemed relieved that I may have an answer. However, she stated tick-borne illnesses falling outside of classic

Lyme disease were not in her area of expertise, and while she could give me the standard twenty-one days of doxycycline, she could not take on treating me long-term for ehrlichiosis or anaplasmosis, the illnesses my symptoms matched with best. This was not a surprise, nor did it upset me. I already had an appointment set up with a Lyme-literate nurse practitioner (LLNP). My PCP was supportive when I told her about the LLNP. She knew someone who had been greatly helped by this same LLNP and was happy for me that I finally had a path forward. I had, for the first time in all those months, a name for my illness. Walking out of her office with a prescription in my hand felt like a hard-won victory.

My first appointment with the LLNP would take place eight days after starting the doxycycline. I was happy to have found a Lyme-literate practitioner and had an intuitive feeling she and I would work well together. Her website described her as both a nurse practitioner (NP) and an herbalist, which felt like a good mix for me as I was always someone who would try plant-based medicine to treat what ailed me, and then move onto Western medicine if need be. I began my course of doxycycline with high hopes for recovery and a feeling the tide had turned.

In those very early days, I looked at the more mainstream information on tick-borne illness: the Mayo Clinic website, the CDC website. I later learned from Pamela Weintraub, a science writer and editor, and many other Lymies, that there is a real disconnect between mainstream information on tick-borne illness and the lived experience of those of us afflicted with it. Based on what I had read thus far, I began my twenty-one days of doxycycline under the impression that twenty-one days was all it would take to eradicate the bacteria that had been running rampant in my body and brain for six months. I was elated at the thought of fully recovering my health in just three short weeks. Unfortunately, I would soon discover that everything I had read on the mainstream medical sites did not apply to those with disseminated tick-borne illness. When the bacterial invaders had time to multiply and spread over the course of multiple months, or years in some cases, treatment looked entirely different.

On the third day of antibiotic treatment my fatigue dramatically worsened to the point where I was bed-bound apart from trips to the bathroom. I had been up for meals and able to do light cleaning and cooking most days, and so the sudden transition back to bed full time was disappointing, especially when I was under the impression I should be getting better soon. On the fifth day of doxycycline treatment, I was propped up on the couch trying to have a conversation with my husband, despite my overwhelming fatigue, when I began to shake. At first the tremors were in my hands, but quickly the vibrating feeling swept through my body and every bit of me began to violently quake. My mouth was thrown open, head thrashing backward and forward, arms and legs thrust out, shaking so hard I began to shimmy lower and lower on the couch at risk of crashing to the floor. My husband looked horrified. The seizure-like activity lasted just a few minutes, and when it stopped, I burst into tears. We'd both been so hopeful I would respond well to the medication and begin to improve, this episode hit us especially hard.

We had the sense this was beyond what my PCP would know about, so we placed a call to the LLNP and an acquaintance, Carrie, who had offered herself as a resource. Carrie had a long history with Lyme disease, which had altered her life dramatically and made her an unfortunate expert on the vagaries of the disease and the treatment. She was the first one to get back to us and informed us that I was having a Jarisch-Herxheimer reaction. Named after the physicians who discovered the phenomenon, it's a reaction to endotoxins produced by the death of certain bacteria within the body at the beginning of antibiotic treatment. It is a common occurrence in the treatment of syphilis and other spirochete type bacterial infections. A Jarisch-Herxheimer reaction involves a whole host of unpleasant symptoms, such as muscle pain, fatigue, rash, fever, and tremors. It is so prevalent that all members of the Lyme disease community have a shorthand for it, calling it a Herx. The only treatment for a Herx is to support your body's ability to flush the toxins through, so Lymies are known to drink a ton of water with lemon, take milk thistle to support the liver's process, lie in hot baths with Epsom salts, and consume binding agents like chlorella to attach to the endotoxins and remove them from the body. In a severe Jarisch-Herxheimer reaction, the patient may be taken off the antibiotic, and then restarted at a lower dose. This is what the nurse practitioner recommended when she called us back. She advised me to stop the medication and assured me we would come up with a new plan when I came into her office.

Thus began my relationship with treatment, which would span the next eighteen months. In the first week I went from the elation of finding a name for my illness and finally being on a treatment, to the demoralizing realization that treatment was not going to be quick. The uncertainty I had lived with for six months was shape-shifting from uncertainty about what had ailed me to uncertainty about what treatment I could tolerate. The bright spot in all of this was that I had places to turn for help now. I was not alone anymore, and that reassurance was invaluable.

My initial visit with the LLNP felt reparative in some way, a much-needed contrast to my experience in the medical world before. She was a kind-faced woman in her early forties, with coppery red hair that she wore in a braid hanging over her shoulder and freckles dotting her skin. The intake session was ninety minutes. She wanted to know my whole story: who I was before the illness, everything that had happened, and all of my thoughts, feelings, and questions about the illness and treatment options. She had already consulted with a Lyme-literate MD about my case to get an initial treatment plan started based on the intake paperwork I had submitted online earlier in the week. She was 100-percent attentive and aghast when I told her about the conversion disorder diagnosis. She was the first person who could explain tick-borne illness to me in a way that was germane to my experience and made sense physiologically.

The LLNP explained I was probably infected at some point in the late summer or early fall, and my immune system was fighting off the infection effectively enough so I only experienced mild fatigue. Then I broke my hand, introducing a physiological stressor, allowing the infection to gain strength. Around the time of my birthday I caught a virus, which diverted my immune system from the bacteria. The first acute symptom of the tick-borne illness (shortness of breath) cropped up as the virus faded, and the treatment for the shortness of breath was steroids, which suppressed my immune system. In the span of four days, from November 4 through 8 I had taken oral, IV, and inhaled steroids. With my immune system effectively suppressed the bacteria ran rampant in my body, focusing their attack on my central nervous system, causing paralysis.

The LLNP speculated that the good antibodies provided by the IVIG and the IV antibiotic treatment killed off some of the bacteria, causing them to recede to the point where I'd appeared to be healthy again. However, the bacteria was not eradicated and began to multiply over the course of my time in acute rehab. By the time I was discharged home I was heading into a major relapse of the bacterial illness.

In the mainstream medical world, my symptoms were treated as a disjointed jumble. Now here I was, getting a connected narrative. It made absolute sense. I had intuitively known that all of these threads were a part of one cohesive picture; I just hadn't been able to name it on my own. My LLNP suggested I go back on the doxycycline but begin at a smaller dose and work my way up to a therapeutic dose over the course of a week. It was reassuring to know there was a way to restart treatment that might avoid the terror of tremors, and the extreme fatigue.

The testing for anaplasma and ehrlichia, still our best bet on what bacteria was affecting me, is expensive, and so we decided to start treatment and go with a basic test for classic Lyme. My LLNP felt comfortable diagnosing a tick-borne illness based on my symptoms. Many Lyme-literate providers think of Lyme and associated diseases as a clinical diagnosis, meaning "diagnosed through the presence of symptoms rather than through testing." This is because the testing is unreliable. In a 2016 study looking at the efficacy of serologic, or blood, tests for Lyme disease, it was found that serologic tests for Lyme disease had only 57.6 percent sensitivity—meaning the testing missed over 40 percent of cases. In the early stages of the disease, sensitivity drops to 46.3 percent (per "The Accuracy of Diagnostic Tests for Lyme Disease in Humans, A Systematic Review and Meta-Analysis of North American Research," an article published in the journal *PLoS One* in December 2016).

The testing for classic Lyme (the borrelia spirochete) came back inconclusive: I did have some of the bands on the Western blot, indicating the presence of the bacteria, but not all of the bands. Given the tenuous nature of the testing, we chose to continue doxycycline as it works for many of the tick-borne illnesses. In addition to the doxycycline, my LLNP started me on supplements to support my body as I dealt with the disease and the treatment. Sadly, when I found the appropriate provider and treatment, it was all outside the mainstream medical system, and therefore none of it was covered by insurance. The LLNP explained she wanted to provide care according to what was best for her patients, as opposed to the care the insurance companies dictated. Therefore, she opted not to bill insurance and was out of network for all patients. The lab providing the most accurate testing for tick-borne illness was also out of network. Because my LLNP was out of network, any medication she prescribed was also not covered. I later learned that most Lyme-literate providers do not take insurance. This is because in states where Lyme is endemic, insurance companies began reporting providers to their disciplinary boards for going outside the standards set by the Infectious Disease Society of America that dictate short courses of antibiotic treatment for Lyme disease. What most people who have had a Lyme infection not treated within the first month of onset know, however, is that the bacteria disseminate in your body, burrowing deep into your tissues, where they obstinately hide out. Disseminated Lyme disease treatment is long and complex—a reality that was just beginning to infiltrate my world.

Thankfully, we still had some savings from the Go Fund Me. I was lucky. So many people affected by tick-borne illness are not so fortunate, and because the set of diseases are often debilitating to the point where a person can't work, many are living in poverty by the time they receive their diagnosis and are unable to afford treatment. Even with the Go Fund Me money, Scott and I were struggling financially, with my inability to work robbing us of 50 percent of our income. We couldn't afford more testing. Knowing it may not even be accurate, we tabled testing and accepted this would be a clinical diagnosis.

In those first couple days after the LLNP visit I was flying high. What I had known deep in my gut was true. My body had been invaded, and my mind was not to blame. I began the process of shaking off the mistrust of my own perceptions that had snaked its way into my psyche when I was diagnosed with conversion disorder. It would take years to fully rid myself of it, to unpack the impact of being dismissed as mentally ill when I was vulnerable and suffering.

There is a type of emotional abuse called gaslighting, when one is told their reality is invalid and only the reality of the dominant party is real, despite evidence to the contrary. Looking back on my journey through the Western medical world, I can see many instances of gaslighting. In the wake of finding a name for my illness, questions frequently arose in my mind. *Why did this happen to me? Is it because I'm female? Is it because we have created conditions where it is unacceptable for doctors to utter the words, "I don't know"?* Whatever the reason, the gaslighting I experienced was nearly as disturbing as the illness itself, adding an unnecessary layer of anguish to an already traumatic situation. In those early days of treatment I felt as if I had been freed from a trap, and I was, but I didn't know that while the door was finally open, the long crawl to reach the outside world would be treacherous and winding.

The diagnosis and treatment of tick-borne illness, in particular Lyme disease, has had a rich history of dysfunction in the United States. One of the first books I read after getting the diagnosis of tick-borne illness was Pamela Weintraub's *Cure Unknown: Inside the Lyme Epidemic*. Weintraub, a science writer and editor, took on the task of trying to untangle why so many people with tick-borne illness are not properly diagnosed within the Western medical system in the US. The story you hear again and again from people who have Lyme disease and other tick-borne illnesses is that they sought help for years, consulting with countless doctors, without getting any tangible assistance. Almost universally Lyme patients have been diagnosed with chronic fatigue syndrome, and when they don't accept the diagnosis and push further, they are labeled as mentally ill. Many, like me, are diagnosed with a conversion or somatic disorder. Many are diagnosed with depression as a way to explain the crippling fatigue that comes with tick-borne illness. Many sufferers of tick-borne illness are diagnosed with an anxiety disorder because they worry about their health. As if their worry is the pathology, not the illness itself. Somehow, it is considered abnormal to be anxious after a long period of debilitating illness without adequate diagnosis and treatment. The end result of all of these misdiagnoses is that people with undiagnosed tick-borne illnesses continue to suffer. Prevailing wisdom by Lyme-literate doctors is the longer a tick-borne illness goes untreated the harder it is to recover from, a reality with which I would soon become painfully acquainted.

We suddenly found ourselves not only navigating the ups and downs of treatment, but also diving into negotiations over out-of-network services with our insurance company, sucking hours and hours of our time and not yielding much in terms of reimbursement. However, the optimism was returning to our home as I restarted treatment without consequence. After building up to a therapeutic dose of doxycycline and staying there for two weeks I began to notice a shift in my energy. I could putter around the house for a bit longer; my mental focus appeared to be improving slightly; and I could follow conversations with a little more ease. I found my rest periods felt more restorative. This gradual improvement continued until mid-June, when the largest shift in my health occurred, and overnight I was astoundingly and miraculously better.

I remember the exact moment I realized that I was in remission. I woke up in my own bed, as I had finally become strong enough to climb the stairs and sleep next to my husband. My eyes sprang open that morning, which was a departure from the murky awakenings I had become accustomed to. I remember taking a deep breath and feeling a charge go through me, like an electrical current, only this was mild and pleasant, unlike the intense buzzing sensation neuropathy had provided me.

I sat up in my usual manner, rolling onto my side and using my arm to push my body upward in an effort to get my weak muscles to respond. However, on this day it took very little effort and I found myself moving with a quickness and ease I hadn't experienced in more than seven months.

I sat on the side of the bed very aware of how different everything felt. I stood and practically ran down the stairs, eager to test this new body out, to see if it was real. I paused in my kitchen, laughing until I cried after making a few laps around the house to convince myself I wasn't just imagining it. My children came down the stairs sleepy-eyed, wondering what all the hubbub was about. I remember drawing them to me and telling them I thought the medicine had worked; I thought I might be better, really better. I remember Scott coming downstairs, his confusion at my laughter and tears, and his pessimism, always his go-to response: "Don't get too excited. We'll see how the day goes."

For me, though, there was no need to wait. The only good thing that had come out of all the gaslighting over the past seven months was that I had learned to trust my intuition about my body. I simply knew I had been restored.

Throughout the next month my momentum built. With a careful reintroduction of activity, I gained strength and was doing things I could not have imagined two months prior. I took my children on full day outings that required me being on my feet for hours. It was the first summer I had been able to be home with them, as I had always had to work full time, and we relished it.

There was a celebratory feeling in our house each and every day. It even affected my husband, who began to laugh and smile easily, who heaped praise on me for the elaborate meals I cooked and the big cleaning projects

I took on. It was a golden time, and while I knew my recovery would mean I would need to return to work soon, I was really enjoying the life of a healthy stay-at-home mom.

Looking back, this may have been the happiest my family ever was. I felt my husband and I had traversed this incredible hardship with grace and love, and in doing so we had somehow repaired the damage done by his harshness in times when he was unwell. I felt a deep sense of forgiveness as I let go of the painful moments that had come before. The kids thrived with all the attention I was able to give them, and the easing of the fear and concern which hung over our house for months made their faces glow. It was a time of connection with friends whom I could now go and see. I could go to the summer potlucks and backyard parties. It was great, and I knew it was special. I am glad I did not take this time for granted, for while I had no way of knowing what was to come, I somehow knew this celebration was something to hold onto.

Chapter 6

In July I began discussions with my LLNP about returning to work. She wanted me to wait until August, and if I was still thriving, to return then. I let my employer know I was considering coming back in August. Finally, a date was set, August 10, and I began to look forward to becoming a hospice social worker again. I had always worked; it is a huge part of my identity. My first job was at a Goodwill store when I was sixteen, and with the exception of my son's infancy, I'd worked ever since. Not working, especially when I was too sick to fully inhabit the homemaker role, made me feel useless. I defined myself as a caregiver: taking care of my hospice patients, my children, my husband. Without my role, I felt lost.

I was also aware of the toll my absence had taken on my colleagues. Our department was small, with just four full-time social workers. With me out, we lost 25 percent of our team. We were supposed to have what is called a PRN social worker who fills in when needed, but after the merger of our small hospital with a larger corporate health system, a policy was implemented where positions were not filled when vacated. Our PRN social worker had quit about six months prior to my illness, and the position was lost to the "savings-through-attrition" policy.

When the day arrived, I found myself excited to be walking through the doors of our main office, where I would spend a day getting reacquainted with the job before I jumped back into the heart of my work, covering the inpatient hospice unit. From the moment I walked into our shared workspace it became clear the nine months of being short-staffed had burned out my colleagues. Mostly, they were incredibly kind and welcoming, celebrating my return to health and work. One colleague was a bit hostile. She was eaten up by stress, and I understood where it was coming from. They had been working with extra-large caseloads and covering the inpatient unit for nine months. I can only imagine how tired they were. We were all aware of the savings-through-attrition policy on hiring. My position would not have been filled if I had been terminated or quit due to my illness. My return from the Lymelands was the only option for my coworkers to get some relief. I was glad I could give that to them now.

I was quickly assigned a small caseload of home-based patients and knew I would be taking all the new assignments for a while. New patients have to be assessed within five days of admission to our hospice program. Assessments require a good amount of time spent with the patient and their family, getting to know them, and an even longer period sitting in front of the computer typing a report out, and checking boxes on an assessment screen. Along with taking new clients coming into the home-based hospice program, I would also be meeting with the patients and families coming into our Hospice House in order to assess them and offer emotional support through the dying process. And I would help families plan for providing care when a patient left our inpatient unit after a stay for symptom management.

I knew I would quickly become busy, but I wasn't worried. I felt great, rested. I was energized by inhabiting the role I knew so well. Most importantly, I got to go back to something I deeply loved: being with people who were facing one of the hardest things life throws at us.

My first new patient was Mary, a woman in her mid-fifties who lived independently in a small home located in a cozy neighborhood in our town. Mary was digesting a lot of difficult information. Up until a few weeks prior she'd been working full time at our local university and was fighting her pancreatic cancer with regular chemotherapy and radiation. A positron emission tomography (PET) scan revealed her cancer had been spreading despite her efforts, and her doctor had given her the brutal news that there was nothing more to be done and it was time to accept a referral to hospice.

I have tried to imagine this transition, how it feels to shift from holding onto and protecting your life, to letting go of it. It seems impossible that people are capable of it. My experience of going on the vent only deepened my respect for my hospice patients, as the will to live I experienced was overwhelmingly strong, single minded, and unrelenting. Yet these hospice patients were not going to live; this was their reality to contend with. I see processing this news as a sort of free fall, your feet stripped of solid ground for a good long while as you assimilate. Mary was free-falling on the day we first met. It became clear to me, within seconds of introducing myself, that Mary was surviving this free fall by being in control of what she could, and I would need to be very aware of allowing her that control. I was tasked with helping her understand what her needs might be at the end of life, and how I could be able to help.

I immediately noticed Mary had a toy box in her living room, and through an open bedroom door I spied a room with more children's belongings. As a social worker, you quickly learn the points of connection, the things people can talk about with ease, and you enter the conversation there. I asked her about the toys and if there was a little one in her life. She lit up when talking about her grandson, a beautiful two-year-old boy. She shared that her daughter was in nursing school and she tried to take her grandson as much as she could. It was clear how much her daughter meant to her.

I could tell Mary had a close-knit family, and this is a relief for a hospice social worker. Isolated patients with estranged families are the very hardest to help, especially if they have limited resources. Patients need a tremendous amount of care at the end of life, and most don't want to end up in a nursing home (I don't blame them). It is a hole in our system of care; we don't have a safety net for these people.

People like Mary still fall through the cracks in several ways. Commercial health insurance and Medicare don't pay for in-home caregivers. Long-term care policies do, but most working-class people can't afford this on top of their health insurance premiums. Medicaid does, but working individuals oftentimes don't qualify for Medicaid until they have left their jobs and been without a paycheck for a month. People with terminal illnesses don't leave their jobs until they are too sick to work, at which point they quickly need care. By the time they even qualify to apply for Medicaid they are quite ill, and then they have to go through the application process, which requires digging up a bunch of documents that often get lost after submission to Medicaid and need to be resent. The state's Family and Social Services Administration office has ninety days to review and approve the Medicaid application. If the terminally ill person is still alive when approval is rendered, they are not immediately eligible for in-home care; instead they go on a wait-list. Most wait eighteen to twenty-four months to get a waiver for in-home care. Even with a waiver, care is no more than forty hours per week, more often much less. So, it falls to family and friends.

I didn't have the sense that Mary had a lot of resources, so to know she had an involved family was a solace. My relief was tempered a bit when we finally got to the core of the conversation: what Mary was going to do when she needed full-time care. This is difficult to consider for patients who are still in free fall. Honestly, I felt like a jerk having to bring it up at this point. Mary had an aggressive cancer, however, and I had seen this type of cancer ravage a body, creating severe symptoms that can transform a walking and functioning person into a bed-bound person in just a few weeks. We needed to start thinking about her care, even if it was scary to do so.

Mary stiffened when I brought it up, understandably, but I persisted. She was adamant her daughter would not be her caretaker. It was obvious to me she wanted to be the one who took care of her daughter until the end, and this was her way of doing it. When pressed, she told me she had some friends out of state who would come and stay with her when it was time, and I could tell it would be unwise to push the conversation any further. As gently as I could, I suggested a few follow-up steps, such as contacting those friends and making sure they would be able to come when needed. I knew as soon as I left, Mary would try to put this conversation as far out of her mind as possible.

I really liked Mary. I admired her independence. I was touched by her love for her grandson and the way her face filled with pride when she talked about how hard her daughter was working. I was sad for her, and her family. Sad for what was to come—the wasting away of her body, the loss of her independence. She had a sharp mind. A good memory. I knew it would be painful for her when her mind became fuzzy from pain meds and disease progression. I hoped her friends really would help, but had seen numerous patients struggle to find aid. I was worried for her, and for me too. As her social worker, I really wanted to honor her wishes around her daughter, but I also knew the chaos of the last weeks or months of a person's life, and how often the ideal is unattainable.

After two weeks, while the stress and pressures of the job took some getting used to, I found myself enjoying the work and feeling strong. My only complaint was about the doxycycline, which I was still taking morning and night. The antibiotic had begun to seriously irritate my stomach. I always took it with food, and yet I was experiencing a burning sensation in my stomach for hours after ingesting it. Despite probiotics, my digestive system was a mess. I had only taken antibiotics a handful of times in my adult life and my body was not prepared for three months of daily interaction with these meds. I went to my LLNP and asked her if I could go off of the antibiotic now that I had been in remission for two months. The mainstream literature recommended a way shorter course of antibiotics, and while I was already figuring out that the mainstream knowledge of tick-borne illness did not often match up to my experience, I still put some stock in it. My LLNP told me both she and the Lyme-literate MD she had consulted with thought I should stay on the antibiotic longer, but ultimately it was up to me, as it was my body.

I couldn't have known how dire the consequences of quitting treatment would be. We all assumed if I began to have symptoms after quitting I would just go back on the meds and all would be well. I made the decision to quit taking the doxycycline.

The first week was a success. The stomach pain quickly went away, and my digestive issues cleared up soon after. I entered the second week off antibiotics feeling good and relieved I seemed to have leapt another hurdle. However, at the end of the second week, near the beginning of September, my energy began to lag. At first I thought it was the long days catching up with me as my caseload grew and the inpatient hospice work began to monopolize my time. Sometime in the second week of September, though, my limbs began to feel heavy in a terrifyingly familiar way. I immediately went back on the doxycycline, hoping to get back to the buoyant place I was at just a month prior. After a week back on it I did not feel any better and was coming home from work too tired to interact with my family.

Scott was worried. He feared I might be sick again and have to quit working. He did not like being the primary breadwinner. It created a lot of pressure for him. I could relate. I had never liked the months when he didn't work due to his depression. I could see the relief my husband experienced when I'd returned to work, and I didn't want to rob him of the experience so quickly.

So I continued to go in, day after day, despite my obvious decline in health. By mid-September my legs began to drag when I walked the halls of our inpatient unit. I began holding onto walls and desktops as I navigated my workspace. I scheduled in-home assessments for the morning so I could be sure my body wouldn't give out in someone's home. It seems ludicrous to me looking back. I should have stopped and rested my body. I can see myself walking to the lunch table in the staff lounge hunched over and dragging my legs with each step because I didn't have the strength to pick them up. In fact, the lunch table at our main office was the site where my body, finally and decisively, quit on me.

I had joined my fellow social workers for lunch after visiting Mary in our inpatient unit. Just as I had feared, the out-of-town friends had not materialized and she had deteriorated quickly, her abdomen filling with fluid, debilitating her and causing her great pain. She had been admitted to our inpatient hospice unit, and I was in the midst of figuring out how to get her care when she was discharged back home. I returned to the main office worried about her, and too distracted to recognize I was pretty weak myself. In fact, a nurse said to me upon my return, after the walk from car to office had clearly wiped me out, that I should consider using a walker. I remember feeling a little indignant at the thought of shuffling around with a walker. I sat at the lunch table unusually quiet, as conversation felt like it would take too much out of me.

One by one, my coworkers finished their food and got up to go back to work. I am a slow eater and was moving especially slow because of my exhaustion, so I was the last person left at the table. When I was finally done, I went to stand up and realized I couldn't. My legs were made of stone, still and heavy under the table, and completely unmovable. The reality I had been trying to avoid crashed down. I was sick again.

I was in shock. For a few minutes I froze. Like fight or flight, freeze occurs when the body faces a threat that totally overwhelms the system. In freeze one stops thinking, acting, and just exists until the brain kicks back in. A few nurses even walked through the staff kitchen while I sat at the table and I didn't think to ask for help or explain my situation. I just sat blank and staring at the wall across from me.

Finally, one of the bereavement counselors, with whom I was close, came through and saw I was still at the table and didn't look right. As soon as she bent over and put herself at eye level with me, gently asking if I was okay, I snapped out of the freeze state and began to convey that I couldn't move my legs and I seemed to be sick again. Immediately, she went to get help. Our office space had both nurses and social workers, so I had several nurses summoned to my side. Of course, because this was a rare tick-borne illness, no one really knew what to do. The consensus was to get a wheelchair and get me to the emergency department, but I knew this course of action would prove useless.

I had a sense of what was wrong with me: I was in a full relapse, and this knowledge was causing me to slowly crumble inside. I was not going to be able to keep it together for much longer and didn't want to have a full, sobbing meltdown in the hospice kitchen, so I asked a couple of my closest colleagues to take me home. My supervisor had entered the scene at this point and gave us all permission to leave. My colleagues moved the table away from me, rolled a wheelchair up next to me, and I used my arms to transfer to the wheelchair, picking my useless legs up one at a time and placing them on the footrests. We then wheeled out to my colleague's car.

With some help I was able to get into the back seat. I sat in silence while we drove the twenty minutes to my house. My colleague tried to reach my husband, but he didn't answer his phone. By the time we got to the house my legs came back online just enough to walk inside while being supported on both sides by my colleagues. I recall being embarrassed because I had been too tired to clean for weeks and the house was a mess. My coworkers helped me lie down on the futon. Suddenly, it all became too much to bear. Finding myself back in this same spot, the place I had been trapped for months, elicited gut-level, body-shaking sobs. Luckily, I was with two hospice bereavement counselors; they were used to people crying.

When I could speak again, I asked them to call my mom, who was working at the Hospice House, our inpatient unit, and see if she could come. She was able to arrive quickly, the whole department now aware of how sick I had become again; another RN was dispatched to cover my mom at the Hospice House. When she arrived my coworkers left us, and she held me while I cried a second time. Then, we dried our eyes, lay down together, and distracted ourselves by watching multiple episodes of *Dancing with the Stars*. My mom held me in her arms the whole afternoon.

Up until this point in my illness, Scott had surprised me in the best of ways. He had traditionally not done well in situations where he perceived any pressure on him. I had learned many gentle back doorways to approach things with him, to avoid the pressure trap over the years. In the past I had watched him back away from difficult situations. So I was really proud of him when he kept showing up for me throughout this hard, scary year. However, my relapse seemed to be too much for him.

It was subtle at first. In all of the various crises up to this point we had reached for each other, and there was a level of intimacy and sense of unity. When Scott came home and learned of my full-blown relapse, he put the internal shutters up. His eyes became distant. I was too tired and overwhelmed at the time to give it much thought, but there was a change inside of me too, a familiar sense of watchfulness that stole over me as Scott's mood began to shift.

The next week involved much discussion with human resources, my supervisor, and the insurance company who held my short- and long-term disability policies. I was placed back on a medical leave, which caused me tremendous guilt. I had noticed in the week before my relapse that my colleagues finally seemed able to relax and enjoy the little bit of breathing space my return had provided them. They were just beginning to believe things would be okay, and then I yanked the carpet out from under them. Of course, in retrospect I can see the carpet was yanked out from under all of us, myself included, but at the time I hadn't had enough therapy to recognize my sense of responsibility for my illness was a bit exaggerated. I felt as though I had personally created this chaos.

I was desperate to fix it. I could not accept that I wasn't just going to take a little more time and come right back. Each day I spent being too sick to work felt like another mark against me. I chafed against the debility. I hated it. I immediately saw my nurse practitioner who wanted to do more testing to pinpoint my exact tick-borne illness. The first round of testing had shown I had antibodies for classic Lyme, and we had gone with doxycycline thinking we could cover other bacterial invaders, because it has a positive effect on most of the tick-borne illnesses. Ticks actually carry many different types of bacteria. Some ticks can transmit multiple infections in a single bite. Since the doxycycline was not working, we needed to be able to define the bacteria and design a treatment plan that was more targeted. With the loss of my income we couldn't afford to pay out of pocket for a broader panel of tests to locate which bacteria was making me sick. We decided to go through my insurance company in hopes of getting coverage for the test. In the meantime I went off all treatment as the doxycycline wasn't doing anything for me and the testing would be more accurate if I wasn't on treatment when I had the blood draw. It took two weeks to go through the insurance company. Really, it was not a long time for the insurance world, but it felt like an eternity to me as I was anxious to get back into treatment.

My nurse practitioner and my primary care doctor both put a lot of time into getting the testing approved, and by the end of the process we were assigned a nurse from the insurance company to manage my case, because we had made so many phone calls. The nurse assigned to us was able to get the test covered.

By the time I had the blood draw, I was zapped of all strength, unable to do basic things, like pick up my kids or go to the grocery store. I was doing everything I could do around the house as I watched Scott becoming more overwhelmed each day. I was back to being up for thirty minutes and down for two hours. I could cook dinner, but by the time I sat down to eat I could barely keep myself upright, and I had to bail on the bedtime routine. This was confusing for the kids. When I was in remission, I had taken over all elements of the household care and the childcare to give Scott a much-deserved break. Now, suddenly, I was absent again. I felt guilty.

After the blood samples were sent in we had to wait another week for the results to come back. When they finally did, I met with my LLNP to go over them. We had done a panel to look for many different types of tick-borne illness, including babesia, bartonella, ehrlichiosis, and anaplasmosis. I was worried none would come back positive and I would be thrown back into the void of uncertainty. That was not the case. My testing came back positive for anaplasma, the sister bacteria to ehrlichia, which had always been our best guess as the symptoms matched so well. Anaplasmosis can also affect the neurological system and cause all of the symptoms I had experienced. Anaplasmosis is in the rickettsia family and is best targeted by certain antimicrobial medications. I was sent off with a prescription for rifampin.

This time around, I thought I was prepared for a Jarisch-Herxheimer reaction. I wanted to jump into treatment at the full dose because I wanted to get better quickly. I was still clinging to the idea I could go back to work, and this felt more and more urgent as Scott was moving into what was clearly a depression. Based on past experience, I feared he would have to stop working at some point. I am not sure anyone could have been prepared for this type of Herx, though.

Within days of starting the rifampin, I was hit with blinding pain. Joint *and* muscle pain. Every tiny movement, from shifting my weight while reclining to even moving a finger caused a cascade of pain that left me breathless and brought tears to my eyes. Even lying still, I felt a constant baseline of pain. It put me back to being a full-time occupant of the futon, and it was the proverbial straw that broke my husband's back.

Scott became irate when I wasn't able to help around the house. One evening, when I told him I couldn't get up to cook dinner, he refused to cook. I remember forcing myself off the futon, each movement resulting in waves of pain, causing a prickle of sweat to break across my forehead, and a wave of nausea. I needed to attempt cooking, my children had to be fed, so I pushed through the pain, onto my feet and into the kitchen. I only got as far as reaching to open the cabinet door to gather ingredients before breaking out into sobs after lifting my arm. I remember standing, my palms flat on the counter, crying and saying to Scott, "I am so sorry. I can't. I am so sorry."

He looked at me with no empathy, just a coldness, indicating he had shut down and there was going to be no understanding. I padded back to the futon and lowered myself, experiencing sheer agony as skin and muscle made contact with the futon, every nerve and fiber releasing pain signals. I don't remember how dinner ended up happening (probably Scott cooked after all), but I do remember terror gripping me when I recognized I had lost his support and there was nothing I could do about it.

Scott's resentment simmered and became a palpable force in our household. My pain plagued me, and nothing seemed to alleviate it. In my memory, this period of pain seems like an eternity, when in reality it was only about ten days. On October 10, I wrote to a friend, "This unrelenting pain is causing me to go to some scary places in my mind. I keep having the thought that this is going to kill me. I feel so afraid every time it crosses my mind. I find myself thinking I have to find an escape. Glad I have no opiates left from the broken hand."

The truth was, I was suicidal. I had wanted to die only once before in my life, when I was seventeen and my body did not conform to the cultural standards of beauty. I was consumed with self-hatred. I took an overdose of opiates after drinking half a bottle of vodka. Thankfully, the suicide attempt was not successful. I slept through the next day and woke up groggy and surprised to find myself still alive. I didn't tell a soul about it until my first experience with therapy a few years later. I was able to process and give voice to my feelings about this attempt, about my body, and my mental health improved.

In October of 2015, I was grateful not to have opiates in the house because I was dangerously desperate to be released from this pain and this body that was failing me, I believed I might do the same thing I did at seventeen. My LLNP tried to help me with gabapentin for the nerve pain, but it didn't do anything for me.

I am not sure how many days I was in pain before a loved one brought me some marijuana. Blessedly, the pot *did* help. After three to four hits I could get up off of the futon and putter around the house for short periods of time. I began doing chores and cooking again, which made life feel a little more anchored, and I began to put my daughter to bed again. I had to smoke every couple of hours to keep up with the pain, but if I stayed ahead of it, the pain was manageable.

I got a bit of a laugh at finding myself a stoner in middle age, but it got me through, and by the last week of October I was moving out of the pain and into a state of slight improvement in my symptoms. It was, as many Lymies experience, a roller-coaster ride. I would have a series of better days, where I could do more, where my brain fog would clear, and I would think I was going into remission again, only to be hit with lethargy, neuropathies, and muscle weakness. Some days I could be the wife and mother I wanted to be. Other days I lay listless on the futon watching hours of bad TV. Scott pulled further and further away from me. Previously, on my bad days he was very attentive, bringing me water, making sure I had healthy snacks nearby, sitting with me and holding my hand. Now, his interactions with me were curt, mostly about what needed to be done around the house. On my bad days I was on my own unless my mom or a friend came by. It was very lonely.

The rifampin treatment continued in this manner throughout November and December. Not enough good days in a row to allow a return to work or a sense of normalcy, and not enough bad days to change course. In trying to ease the strain on Scott, I took over all the housework and childcare again, despite how I struggled. Every day was carefully orchestrated to allow me to do the things I needed to, with necessary rest breaks so my limbs would stay online. My mom came and helped when she could. Our meals were simple, but I was doing it. It was a slog, this period of time. I deluded myself into thinking I could avoid being the target of Scott's irritability if I kept up with everything at home, so I tried hard to do so. I was exhausted all the time and felt the joy drain out of my life. I would escape into TV shows that were simple and easy to follow when my exhaustion forced me to lie down, as this illness rendered me incapable of complex thought. *Dancing with the Stars* and *Project Runway* were go-to shows for me.

I know now I was dissociating frequently throughout this time period, mentally checking out, because the reality of what was happening to me was overwhelming. I faked enthusiasm when the kids came home from school and did my best to force my sluggish mind to follow everything they said to me. I felt I needed to be everything for them as Scott drifted further into his malaise. It was a lot—too much—but what choice did I have?

Part II

Chapter 7

I know so much more about bipolar disorder today than I did in the fall of 2015. I thought I knew it intimately, as we had cared for Scott's mother throughout the last brutal years of her bipolar illness before her death in 2012. Scott's mom, Beth, had been disabled by the disorder. It had manifested at age twenty-one after giving birth to her first child in 1968, Scott's older sister, Sarah. Apparently, the descent into illness happened very quickly, as Scott's father Jim illustrated when he shared the story with me.

One day when Sarah was two weeks old Jim woke up to a normal scene. Beth was tending to Sarah, feeding her and changing her diaper. She then sat with him and had coffee, and he went off to work believing everything in his home was fine. At about 2:00 p.m. he got a call from a staff member at the hospital where Sarah had been born. The person on the other end of the line informed him Beth was there, and she was insisting someone at the hospital had stolen her baby. She was loud and frantic. In fact, Beth had left Sarah at home unattended. Jim, totally unnerved by the call, assumed Beth must have left Sarah with someone and went first to the hospital to gather his wife. But when they arrived home, he realized that Sarah was entirely alone, crying inconsolably.

He was able to quickly get Beth hospitalized and she was diagnosed with manic depression, what we now know as bipolar disorder. Jim was undone by Beth's illness. He genuinely loved her, and the personality changes brought on by her illness broke him. Jim began to drink and retreated into narcissism born out of overwhelm. Empathy was too painful, so he just stopped experiencing it. He was adamant about not having a second child. However, Beth surreptitiously quit taking her birth control and had Scott in 1970. They were both ill-equipped to raise Sarah and Scott, Beth because of her debilitating mental illness, and Jim because of his self-centered nature and fondness for beer.

Beth's first manic episode began a thirteen-year cycle of manic and depressive episodes that transformed her personality. Beth, when stable, was a kind and gentle soul, the type of person who would never curse or say a harsh word toward anyone; a homemaker who enjoyed her children. Mania turned her into an aggressive and sexual being. Scott, Jim, and Sarah shared detailed memories of Beth becoming violent with people. In one instance she attempted to abduct a woman at knifepoint. She repeatedly threatened to kill Jim in front of the children, once while brandishing a large kitchen knife. I had seen Beth in this state, and although she was a tiny woman, she was frightening. Beth, when stable, was a chaste woman. In all my years of knowing her I never once heard her allude to anything remotely sexual while she was in a healthy place mentally. Yet Beth was so promiscuous with strangers when manic that her doctor performed a hysterectomy in the mid-1970s so she would not become pregnant from those trysts.

Scott's childhood was tumultuous. He and Sarah were frequently loaded into the car and sent to stay with their grandparents when Beth was manic. When Beth was depressed, they were left at home to fend for themselves while Beth spent her days in bed. Jim was not a natural caregiver and wasn't able to compensate for Beth's periods of illness. Sarah and Scott essentially raised each other and were close when they were growing up. They both struggled in their own ways, but Sarah's struggles were easier to recognize, and she was able to get therapy and external support. In her mid-teens she moved out of the home and in with her grandparents, leaving Scott on his own right around the time Jim and Beth divorced, when Scott was thirteen.

Beth had a twenty-year period of stability after divorcing Jim, who was, by the accounts of both his children, verbally abusive and self-centered. Her illness, and the medication that helped her manage it, however, stunted Beth. She was challenged when it came to running a home by herself, and after the divorce she heavily relied on Scott to be the adult in the household. He took care of his mom and never stopped playing the role of her caretaker.

In 2003, Beth began having medical problems. She lived by herself in a small apartment, in a major city an hour and a half north of our home. Scott and I decided it would be easier to help her navigate her doctor's appointments and tests if she were living in the same town as us. After moving to our little college town, Beth had her first manic episode in twenty years. This kicked off a terrible ten years of frequent manic episodes that Beth tried desperately to control with medication. Lithium had given her stability, but it had also damaged her internal organs, and she found herself unable to properly metabolize the medication she needed to stay sane.

Scott and I cared for her the best we could—helping her get Medicaid and disability, taking her to doctor's appointments to address her kidney failure, her pancreatitis, her brain abnormalities. We embraced her, and we weathered the manic episodes, where she screamed and cursed and demanded money from us. We had to call the police to our little bungalow when she showed up in the middle of the night, loud and threatening, while our young son slept upstairs. Finally, after years of being in and out of the psych unit, she was sent to a state hospital. It took two years for the doctors there to stabilize her. She was discharged to a nursing home where she died just a few months later, at age sixty-two. It was 2012; our kids were two and seven. Her cause of death was unclear. The impact of her illness, and the medication used to treat it, seemed to be the cause. Her brain malfunctioned first, causing her to lose the ability to speak, and then her body shut down. It was the closing to a long and awful chapter in her life, and ours.

I had lived through long bouts of depression with Scott and one manic episode that occurred when I was pregnant with our daughter. I thought I knew what bipolar disorder looked like in Scott, and I felt I had an extensive knowledge of the disease after caring for Scott's mom. However, what I now know to be a mixed episode of bipolar illness was unrecognizable to me that fall. Scott was swinging between depression, which looked like lethargy, overwhelm, and sadness, to a mental state in which he was frantic, anxious, and most of all irritable. He was electrified by the pressure to provide and kept taking more and more construction jobs despite the fact he was already working over capacity. We had the same conversation again and again where I would tell him he *could not* take another job, and then I would hear him on the phone taking another job. He seemed out of touch with reality at times, as if our constraints didn't exist. Then he would have moments where everything would crash down on him, crush him. He'd have days where he would work into the wee hours, and days where he couldn't leave the house. It was confusing and scary. He was almost always in a bad mood, but it would change from an exhausted bad mood to a wired bad mood. The wired bad moods were the worst, because he could fly into a rage at any second, the tiniest thing setting him off.

At some point in November Scott became convinced that I could do more than I was doing around the house and insisted I could work if I put my mind to it. I knew this wasn't true because an outing to pick up a few things at Target would put me in bed for the rest of the afternoon. I still required rest after just an hour of light housework. If I pushed myself beyond this threshold, my arms and legs would stop working altogether.

He was relentless in his criticism, noting chores I hadn't completed and continuing to point out social work job openings. Scott treated me with contempt when I tried to tell him about my symptoms, as if he didn't believe me. He would refuse to do things I was too weak to do, like carry wood in for the fire, because he didn't believe I was too weak. I would end up doing these tasks, so in some ways he was correct that I could do them. But what would have taken him five minutes would take me an hour and leave me with profoundly weak limbs, requiring hours of rest to recover the use of my body.

If my day was eaten up recovering from a physical task, he would be upset I hadn't done laundry or gone to the grocery store. Sometimes he would scream at me, mostly about housework. One December day I was sitting on the floor tending the fire when he burst into the room screaming at me about some household chore left undone. He was towering over me, his face turning red from the force of his yelling. I froze. I sat stock still barely breathing, and I had the sense that I was suddenly not in my body, as if I were watching our two figures from afar. I remember wishing I could just disappear, but there was no escape. Everything I said just seemed to further infuriate him. I feared he might hit me. It was the first time I remember being truly frightened of him.

The intensity level of his rage was something new. In the past, periods where he targeted me and tore me down were followed by "honeymoon" periods where he'd apologize and build me back up. Between October 2015 and April 2016, he rarely apologized for his rages. I tried to talk with him about it when he seemed calm, but he would become enraged all over again, or act as if he had no idea what I was talking about. In years past I had the sense he was in control of his anger, using it as a tool to express himself, or get my compliance. It was hurtful, but not frightening. Now the rages felt uncontrollable. I had never worried about Scott becoming violent with me in the past. Now I did.

He could not see the ways in which he was hurting people. I had compassion for him, even though I was deeply hurt by how he was treating me, because I could imagine how difficult it was to have a disabled spouse. He was providing for our family by himself, while having children to care for. I also knew he had cared for his mother since age thirteen and was possibly feeling grief and rage over being thrust into this role again. I felt guilty for putting him through it. I internalized this, holding myself responsible for being sick.

Scott also disengaged from participating in my treatment. He quit going to doctor's appointments with me and seemed disinterested in my recovery, except for figuring out how to get cheaper meds. I had been on a waiting list to see the Lyme-literate MD (LLMD) who had been consulting on my case since June 2015. In March 2016 I finally had an appointment to see her. I wanted Scott to attend the appointment with me, as I was hopeful this doctor would be able to talk with him about my limitations, but he refused to go. I had been placed on a second, rotating antibiotic to complement the rifampin and was taking a whole slew of supplements. My medical care alone was a lot to manage, given I had to take medications and supplements four times per day. I had a pillbox that made me feel like a geriatric patient.

My LLMD changed my antibiotics again and would keep me rotating through different types. In April 2016, my health finally began to improve slightly, but things at home had completely devolved. Scott's rages were more frequent and unpredictable. I was walking on eggshells constantly. One of the things I am most ashamed of is that my children were now also being screamed at, and instead of protecting them, I would coach them on how to avoid setting their dad off. As if we actually had any control over it.

Scott was erupting with hostility in conversations with his customers as well, which I had never known him to do. It was clear something was very wrong, but I couldn't get him to talk with me about it, and I couldn't get him to slow down or engage in any type of self-care. He acknowledged he was stressed from working crazy hours and having so much to tend to, but he would not admit his behavior was out of the ordinary. I knew something bigger was going on.

While I had a whole network of trusted friends and family, Scott's support system was very limited. His sister Sarah lived in Montana, and while they had a pleasant relationship, he didn't open up to her. His father was difficult to talk to—even on a good day, always bringing the conversation back to himself and his grievances, so he was not a likely candidate for support. Scott had several good friends who would have gladly held space for him to talk, but Scott was too private to share his troubles. He refused to talk to anyone but me, and I was too sick and exhausted to be of much support. Sometimes I was too hurt or frightened to open my heart to him.

It was as if, in his mind, I was betraying him by becoming too ill to properly support him. I had always provided the emotional labor in our relationship, coaxing his fears and emotions out of him. His own behavior was driving a wedge between us, and yet at the same time, he seemed furious at me for abandoning him.

On April 9, 2016, the day of my daughter's sixth birthday party, Scott was absolutely wonderful; helpful, kind, energetic, praising me for my efforts. When we awoke the morning after her birthday things seemed as good as they had the day before. Scott went to mow the lawn and I took care of the kids inside. Scott came back in while I was making pancakes, a Sunday tradition. The kids sat at the kitchen table eager for breakfast. I could tell the moment Scott crossed the threshold into the kitchen he was angry, and I felt myself shrink as I stood at the stove, hoping to go unnoticed. Looking for some tea to make, he opened a cabinet. Immediately he began complaining about the dirty state of the cabinet and about how I was letting our house "go to shit." He asked in an angry hiss, "Why don't you care that our house is always filthy?"

Passivity had become a tool to avoid further confrontation, and while I cringed inside hearing myself utter the words, I said, "I'm sorry. I'll try to do better." He replied I could start by cleaning out the cabinet. I told him I would get to it when I was done making the kids their breakfast.

It was then he exploded.

He screamed, "You never do anything I ask you to do. You leave it all to me," as he began pulling out the contents of the cabinet, slamming each item on the counter. I tried to explain I just needed to finish the pancakes (one was in the pan cooking at that very moment), but it seemed to further anger him and he began to throw the contents of the cabinet across the room, all the while screaming about how I was useless and couldn't do anything. How I didn't care about him or my kids and allowed us to live in squalor.

His face was red. His voice was loud. He was close. At certain points in his rant he would put his face near mine, his spit hitting my cheek. Again, I feared he might hit me. Nothing I could say would calm him. He was completely irrational. After I got the pancake out of the pan, I tried to take over the cabinet-cleaning to assuage him, but it was as if he couldn't see me. He ignored my offers to take over, and so I went about getting the kids their pancakes, putting syrup on them, laying out forks, all while being screamed at. The kids sat in shocked silence. When he was finally finished, he stormed outside.

I realized I had barely been breathing the entire time, and when I came back to my breath, I felt myself tremble all over. I was so scared. I looked at my children's faces, and instead of making excuses for Scott, which I had been doing for months, I told them no one should ever be talked to like that. It was as if some survival instinct had finally awoken in me and suddenly I knew whatever this was, it would just get worse, and I needed to get out.

Without giving it any thought, I hurried up the stairs and started packing. I put clothes for three days in a bag for myself and the two kids. When I came down the kids had eaten their pancakes. I grabbed my pillbox and told the kids to get their shoes on—we were leaving right now. After grabbing my phone, purse, and keys, we exited the house.

Scott was mowing the side yard, and I didn't even pause to tell him we were leaving. I just ushered the kids into the car and got into the driver's seat. Scott noticed I was backing up and came next to the car to ask me where I was going. I locked the doors and rolled down the window just two inches before telling him I was going to my parents' house. With no further explanation I pulled away. I can't tell you what I was thinking; it was just instinctual. I was acting on the need to get my children to safety. I remember feeling numb as we unloaded at my mom and dad's house; numb as I explained to my parents in private why we were there. There was a sense of disbelief, *how had this become my life.*

I had hoped my leaving would communicate to Scott the impact of his ongoing verbal abuse and wake him up. It wasn't my intention to leave the marriage, and I texted him within a few hours to make that clear. I simply needed a break so I could feel safe to talk through things with him. Scott did not understand this and told me I had hurt him. He conveyed that I wasn't being supportive of him at a time when he was stressed and overextended.

Over the next two days we had phone conversations where he expressed his anger and frustration at my leaving, and I kept repeating I would like to come home but needed him to be calm and rational before I could. He demanded I apologize to him for leaving. This time I just couldn't apologize; the survival instinct inside of me wouldn't allow it. He was unable to take any accountability for his outbursts and insisted I was overreacting. I was scared to come home while he was still in this state of anger and agitation. Then he quit communicating with me altogether. We were at a stalemate.

On the fourth day of my absence, he called and said if I wasn't home that day he was going to the courthouse the following day to file for divorce. At this point, I felt utterly defeated. He wasn't going to make any attempt to reign in his abusive behavior, and I knew I couldn't manage a divorce at this juncture. The kids and I were living in a cramped bedroom in my parents' house, there was no room for our things, and while my parents were caring for me beautifully, I was already tired of being there. I still wasn't well enough to work and knew I couldn't support a household. I asked him to sit down with me and talk things through.

At first he refused, stating this was who he was and talking about it wouldn't change anything. Finally, he agreed to talk to me if I came home to our house to have the conversation. It was clear when I arrived that he had cycled from an agitated place to a depressed place. He was tearful when he said, "You walked out on me when I needed you the most." He told me how abandoned he felt. I ended up holding him while he lay in my lap on the couch. Seeing his pain and vulnerability stopped me from putting the boundaries in place that I needed in order to feel safe. It was an old pattern for us. Me, letting go of the things I needed to address in our relationship because he was unable to engage in a healthy way. Me, allowing my compassion for him to transcend everything else. He never acknowledged that for months he had been raging at me, criticizing me, and that my concerns were reasonable. I was scared to continue to press the issue because I didn't want him to file for divorce.

So I moved back in. While I couldn't fathom being a divorced single mom at this moment, too sick to work and take care of a home by myself, I did make myself a promise. I promised myself when I could, when I was financially and physically stable, I would leave him.

Much to my surprise, given that Scott refused to acknowledge his verbal abuse, the abuse did stop after I came back. Scott appeared to be in the familiar place of depression but pushed through each day, worked long hours, and appeared constantly overwhelmed. I kept our homelife going the best I could and focused on my recovery. I thought the added strain of my illness had been the cause of all our recent troubles. I think attributing the abuse to something that felt more in my control allowed me to feel as if I had more power in the situation. I quickly put the rages of the previous months away and tried to forget they happened, while simultaneously attempting desperately to prevent any more.

As my family tried to find equilibrium in late spring/early summer, I was beginning to gain ground with my recovery from anaplasmosis. By April I felt as if I could begin to think about working again but knew it would have to be something very flexible. I had been through multiple remissions and relapses and knew the next remission may not last. Because I had finally accepted that I could not return to my full-time job at Hospice, I officially quit. I was not well in April, continuing to experience crippling fatigue, but the neurological symptoms were slowly fading and I sensed I might be on the road to recovery.

I scheduled a date to take an exam for a clinical license. I planned to open a private practice as a licensed clinical social worker (LCSW) providing mental health counseling. I hoped this would be the right fit for my life's limitations. I took the exam in May and passed. Scott and I decided it would make sense for me to care for the kids again over summer vacation, as we would pay more for both of them in day camps than what I could earn just starting out. Meanwhile, I began the work of locating office space, finding a professional to help me create contracts with insurance companies, and purchasing all the necessary equipment and insurance.

As the weeks passed and my business plans were coming together, my health improved greatly, and at my early June visit with my Lyme-literate MD, we decided I would switch from antibiotic therapy to supplements only in mid-June. I was able to make the switch successfully, and then in July added in a special diet for those afflicted with Lyme and associated illnesses. Within a few weeks of starting the diet the last vestiges of the illness, the fatigue and brain fog, began to lift.

In August I started to finally feel as if I were coming back to myself, and I looked forward to my children going back to school and my return to professional social work. I imagined I would open my business slowly, cautiously testing the waters this time instead of diving back in as I had done a year ago.

Overnight this strategy became impossible. Scott descended into a deep depression. He became suicidal, and was often tearful, locking himself in the bathroom to cry. He was unable to work, eat, or sleep through the night. I realized I would have to step into the role of primary breadwinner and accelerated the opening of my private practice. I finally talked Scott into going to a walk-in clinic where he was diagnosed with depression. He was given a prescription for an antidepressant he would end up not taking. My heart hurt for our children, watching one of their parents crash again.

Later that month I went with my daughter to her first-grade open house. When her new teacher asked about her family, my daughter responded, "I have a brother who goes to this school too. My mom can stay home with me now because she is sick, and my dad cries in the bathroom a lot." As if it were totally normal to have a mom who is sick, and a dad who is depressed. It was all she really knew. It made my stomach bottom out, hearing the description of our family. My son became lost in the world of his favorite computer game, Minecraft, in his efforts to escape our reality. I hoped school would offer him some respite from our heavy home.

Scott's way of tackling his mental health issues was to redesign his life. Scott decided to go back to school and quickly enrolled in an online forestry program. He didn't ask for my feedback, and I didn't offer it, but I was secretly angry with him for finally having an official diagnosis of a mood disorder and continuing to refuse therapy and medication. However, I was pretty sure he had been misdiagnosed. While his rages had been hard for me to define as bipolar related, I had seen him experience a distinct manic episode in the past, when I was pregnant with our daughter, and I believed bipolar disorder was the problem.

I was relieved he hadn't taken a drug that could cause mania. The right medication for bipolar disorder is often a mood stabilizer, like Depakote, with the ability to keep both ends of the mood spectrum in check. An antidepressant by itself can sometimes propel someone into mania by only stabilizing the low, without putting a cap on the high. I knew I had no control over Scott's mental health treatment, so I decided to step back and see if his solution would work.

In September 2016, I had everything in place to open my practice, Marabai Rose Counseling. I rented a sweet little office not far from my home, and I was thrilled to discover individual therapy came easily to me. All those years of talking to clients about their losses paid off. I began with a handful of clients but found each week I was adding a couple more, until my practice actually started to earn some income. It was such a relief not being solely dependent on Scott, and I relished my growing sense of confidence. After months of being criticized, I needed to feel there was an arena where I could shine, and this was it.

During this renewal of my career I could have begun taking steps toward leaving Scott. I had made a promise to myself to get out when it was financially feasible. I'd opened my therapy practice and the business took off quickly. I knew I would soon be at a point where I could financially support myself and my children. I didn't go as far as separate bank accounts in setting up my financial independence, but knowing I could earn enough to support us felt freeing. I began seeing a therapist to explore the question, *Should I leave Scott?* I spoke about this freedom in therapy. I recognized being married to Scott was a choice, and I could choose differently. Yet, I couldn't shake the feeling that leaving Scott would be wrong due to his fragility.

I thought back to his last depression; I remembered how tenuous his grip on life seemed then. I thought about the many episodes of depression I had seen him through over the years. I knew he loved me deeply, even if he couldn't always treat me well, and I imagined a divorce would ruin him. My therapist pointed out that my reasons for not leaving my marriage always revolved around what was best for Scott, or the kids, but where was I in the equation? Why didn't I value my own happiness?

I was in the midst of sorting out those questions when Scott began to rearrange things in his life. He appeared happier and was treating me and the kids well, and I thought maybe, just maybe, the thing I had always wished for was happening. A part of me felt it was possible Scott would heal his wounds from childhood and face his family history of mental health issues, and we could be a happy family. Another part of me recognized he wasn't in therapy and working on these issues in a direct way, and without focused effort, healing was unlikely. I talked for hours in the therapy room about it, weighing the pros and cons, but always deciding in the end I wanted to keep our family intact. Even while actively facing these issues, I continued to protect myself with a layer of denial. I was unable to see the full impact of Scott's instability and verbal abuse. To recognize how hurt I really was would have made it hard to function, hard to hold us all together.

I felt incredibly attached to the idea of family. When Scott was in a good place, we had many joyous, authentically connected experiences with our kids. It felt like a huge thing to give up. Also, I couldn't fathom any more life changes. My life had been in chaos for nearly two years, and now my days were peaceful. I wasn't ready to dismantle my family when we were just catching our breath. There was a part of me that disagreed, a voice inside of myself reminding me of the wounds that were still there, unhealed. I shut that voice down. I couldn't move forward into this new phase without burying my wounds, so down they went. I rationalized Scott's abusive behavior by attributing it to the stress my illness had put us all under. I hoped my good health would prevent Scott from spiraling into rage again.

Throughout the rest of 2016 my focus shifted to my burgeoning sense of well-being. My motto was "onward and upward." Up I went, gaining clients, enjoying my life again, and emerging from the fog. It was joyful, and yet there she was, locked away, my internal wisdom. She would bang on the door from time to time when I thought about Scott and the promise I'd made to myself to get out. I couldn't allow myself to hear her knock. Instead, I enjoyed living in a body that functioned. I enjoyed mothering my children. I enjoyed connecting with the woman I used to be.

Chapter 8

My hope for safety and stability seemed to have manifested. Scott and I had a peaceful beginning to 2017. His annual winter depression never happened. He was finding success in his online program through Oregon State University studying environmental science. His grades were excellent, and he seemed happier than he had for a long time. Also, we got to make a lot of beaver jokes, which was good fun. The kids were thriving, happy to have their mom back, returned from the Lymelands. Happy to have their dad stable and kind again. I joyfully baked birthday cakes in March and April. My son turned twelve, my daughter seven.

In the early summer, after nine months of stability, Scott's mood began to shift. At first the shift seemed positive. He was full of energy, excitedly planning a trip for us to go to the West Coast. He began staying up late, looking at dozens of state parks and attractions. He would be up early too, happy to show me the gems he had uncovered as I was sipping my morning coffee. I was glad to see him so enthusiastic. It was so different from the summer before, the summer of crying in the bathroom.

Just two weeks before our departure date I fell off a piece of playground equipment while out with my daughter and broke my ankle. Scott and I were both disappointed by the potential this had for ruining our trip. Yet I was surprised by the extent to which my injury had enraged him. He refused to stay with me when he turned up at the hospital the day of my accident, obviously frustrated. He took our daughter and went home. For some reason they had not given me anything for pain in the hospital, and I was anxious about driving while hurting so badly. When I called Scott to ask for a ride home, he refused to come and pick me up. When I told him I also needed his help because I had meds to get on the way home, he insisted I could drive myself to the pharmacy and pick up my pain meds and then come home. With no other options, I drove myself to the pharmacy. I hobbled in on crutches and discovered a very long line. I waited, while each passing minute on my feet made my ankle throb in a hot rhythm. Finally, I couldn't take it anymore and I got myself to the car and drove home.

When I came in Scott didn't greet me or ask how I was. When I asked him to please go to the pharmacy to get my pain meds, he was furious. When he returned from the pharmacy, he threw my pain medication at me. The next few days he refused to help me with anything as I navigated the world with a broken ankle. I was totally bewildered by his behavior. The previous months had been great. He had been helpful and romantic. I had been supportive of his endeavors at school, and we were both proud of his straight A's. In July it was as if I were dealing with an entirely different person. Scott badgered me about the trip, insisting I needed to decide about whether I could go, but also insisting he wouldn't help me if I went. I was uncertain about going with him in this state, but eventually I decided to move ahead with it.

We went on the trip, and Scott was erratic, swinging from irritated and critical to pleased and joyful. Toward the middle of the trip was an incident where Scott became suddenly irate because our children had begun to play with each other in the back seat of the rental car while it was parked in our campsite. He had told them earlier the car wasn't for playing in. He approached the open door to the back seat, yelling at the kids to get out. My daughter's foot had become trapped in between the seat and a cooler, preventing her from moving quickly. She was trying to tell Scott her foot was stuck, but he was in a blind rage, ordering her to move now, not hearing her. I was moving toward them by this point, trying to get Scott's attention to explain to him that she was stuck when he shoved our daughter forcefully. Her ankle twisted away from her body when he pushed her back. Scott had injured her. I was stunned. Scott had never laid a hand on either of our kids.

She was still crying from shock and pain a couple of minutes later, after I had gone to comfort her and taken her out of the car. Scott approached us, as we stood in our campground. He got down at eye level with our daughter. I thought he might be coming to apologize. Instead his eyes hardened, and his voice was harsh as he ordered, "Stop crying." At that point my daughter began to cry harder, confused and scared about what was happening. At this, Scott reared up to his full height and raised his hands as if he was going to push her down a second time onto the hard earth of the campsite. I screamed at him, *"Don't you touch her!"* throwing myself in between them. This all took place with the other campers just forty feet away, trying to pretend they weren't witnessing child abuse.

I was so ashamed to have strangers overhear this. Scott became livid with me, for what he said was an overreaction. He insisted I was the one making everyone think there was something wrong with our family. He remained big, and loud, and angry. The kids and I retreated into quiet confusion. He took the rental car, leaving us stranded at the campsite until late at night, with no means to get dinner out as we had planned. The kids and I ate road snacks and went to bed. I heard Scott crawl into his sleeping bag around midnight and pretended I was asleep. The following morning Scott was still in the grips of silent rage. He conveyed his anger through every movement as we packed the tent and gear and got on the road.

Finally, he turned to me and hissed, "How could you do that to me? You are ruining this trip for everyone. You need to apologize."

I knew this was a twisted version of what had happened. I knew it wasn't me who was ruining this trip, but I also knew his state of mind. No matter what I said or did, he would see his version of reality, never mine or the kids'. If I didn't capitulate, he would continue to escalate. It had frightened me when he crossed the line into physically hurting one of us; that had never happened before.

I drifted as far away from my body as I could while I whispered, "I'm sorry. Can you forgive me?"

We sat with Scott's anger for most of the drive until finally he began to relax, to warm up, and then as soon as we could we all stuffed the previous day's events into deep storage. The trip continued in this manner—Scott at times warm and excited about taking the kids to search for sea creatures in the tide pool, and sometimes set off by the tiniest thing and shaking with fury.

When we arrived home, I spent the first two weeks of August trying to sort out my feelings in therapy. I wasn't ready to leave quite yet, but I was close. When I told my therapist about the incident with my daughter, she told me she may have to report it to the Department of Child Services because what had happened was clearly child abuse. Eventually, in consultation with her supervisor, she decided not to report it, but I was shaken. I asked Scott to go to couples counseling with me, and in the last two weeks of August we had two sessions in which Scott refused to acknowledge his behavior as abusive, but did acknowledge he had been under tremendous stress during my illness and was behaving in a way he didn't feel good about. It felt like a start, but I was still deeply uncertain about our future together.

As Labor Day approached, I made plans with my best friend Hannah to spend some time at my parents' land out in the country. I needed her counsel and her kindness. My parents and their closest friends had created an intentional community in 1976, the year I was born. My high school friends called it "the hippie ranch." It was over three hundred acres of hilly land in a rural corner of our county. We didn't move out there until I was in my early teens, but we spent most of our weekends and summers there as I was growing up. The community was a family, a network of brothers and sisters, aunts and uncles; and now we had a third generation of children being brought up connected to the community. Hannah brought her two-year-old daughter, and it was a joy to see our children playing and laughing together amongst the hippies in a similar fashion to how we were raised.

I returned home on the Sunday of Labor Day weekend relaxed and sleepy after being out on my parents' land. It had been a nice break from the turmoil in my marriage. My seven-year-old daughter was exhausted after a day in the sun, and my twelve-year-old son was happy to be reunited with his computer. Hannah and her daughter were spending the night with us at the bungalow before returning home the following day.

Hannah and I were plotting our bedtime strategy to maximize the glass of wine and heart-to-heart we were looking forward to after the kids went down. I was so focused on this mission I didn't immediately pay much attention to Scott when I entered our kitchen. He was staring at the screen of our laptop in his usual post since beginning his online program the year before.

With wine on my mind, I lugged the bags and cooler from the car. I had just opened the fridge to start putting the food away when Scott turned to me. As soon as I saw his face, I knew something wasn't right. He looked as if he had seen something terrible, and I remember going through a quick list of possibilities: someone had died; he was going to drop out of school; we were in debt.

He spoke first: "Can we talk outside?"

"Sure," I said, my stomach dropping.

"Where is your cell phone?" he asked in a frightened whisper.

"In my purse," I answered.

"Good," he said, then walked to our front porch. I quickly asked Hannah to oversee toothbrushing and bedtime stories.

I followed Scott onto the porch. He took his cell phone out of his pocket and buried it beneath a pile of camping mats we kept out front. As he tucked it away, I noticed there was electrical tape covering the camera lens and microphone. I took a seat on our porch swing and thought Scott might sit next to me, but instead he began to pace as the words poured out of him.

"I have to tell you something," he began. "I am being watched, they are listening in the house, that's why we have to talk out here. They can hear us through the computer, and they bugged my phone. They have been watching me for weeks. I wasn't sure until a couple of days ago." He paused, and I felt myself going numb. Shock taking over. Dread replacing the ease I had found in the sunshine that day. Scott returned to pacing and ranting. I stared at Scott, taking in his eyes, the staccato beat in his speech, the frantic movement of his body. An image of his phone with tape on it flashed into my mind. *He is psychotic.* As soon as I thought the words, I knew it was true. There was no doubt. Scott was in the grips of psychosis.

I had seen plenty of psychosis when I worked as a tech on the psychiatric unit of our local hospital: patients frightened and unreachable. Trapped in their delusions. I had seen my husband's mother in a state of psychosis, terror stricken, believing someone was coming for her with a shotgun. Frantically trying to usher us out of the house because at any moment they would burst through the door to kill us all.

His look, his energy, was exactly the same. I knew without needing to hear another word, and yet all I could do was listen as he poured out his psychotic tale of persecution. He believed he was being stalked by a group of local women; he called them "gander stalkers." They'd targeted him because he'd looked at pornography online.

He said he was entrapped by one woman in particular, who looked at him with interest at a summer party two months before. He confessed he'd become obsessed with her, pulling up her Facebook page multiple times per day, and had reached out to her twice, trying to arrange a meeting in the hopes of starting an affair. He said the gander stalkers were waiting for this, the reaching out. It triggered the commencement of the gander stalking, and now they were watching his every move, hacking his accounts, sending him messages. He had seen messages from them today on every website he visited and his Facebook account, and he knew they were tracking his phone.

He'd figured out how they communicate, through a Craigslist haiku page where they sent each other coded messages. He cracked the code and knew they were planning on destroying him. He hadn't been able to sleep for the past two nights because he was so worried about it.

The clinical part of my brain began to whir. Heightened sexual impulses, paranoid delusions, sleeplessness, tangential and rapid speech—these were all symptoms of a full-blown bipolar manic episode. In this moment of recognition, there was also minor relief. It was as if a puzzle I had slowly been working on for years was finally complete. Scott was undeniably bipolar. There was no calling this *anger* or *feeling bummed* or *uptight* as Scott had referred to his own moods so often, even after I tried to give him words like *depression* and *anxiety*. His earlier manic episode in 2009 had been confusing. He stayed up all night researching global warming and quit working. He behaved erratically and raged at me. He talked about the mass extinction of the human race in graphic detail in front of our four-year-old, insisting my son needed to understand it. Yet, global warming was a real problem. Plenty of rational people were upset and scared about it and working really hard to stop it. There was nothing then that clearly crossed the line into madness. This time, with the gander stalkers, it was crystal clear that he was experiencing paranoid delusions. Scott was bipolar, and right now he was manic and psychotic and scared out of his mind. The puzzle was complete. I needed a plan.

I knew getting Scott to a hospital was of utmost importance, and near to impossible. Even when not psychotic, Scott was irrational when I tried to get him to access mental health care. Now, he absolutely believed the crisis he was experiencing had to do with being stalked and harassed, and he was not going to be able to put this in a framework of mental illness. I sat with one ear still listening to his rambling tale, while also rehearsing possible pleas for hospitalization.

Finally, he looked at me, eyes pleading, and said, "What do you think I should do?"

"I think we need to get you somewhere you will be safe," I replied.

"There is no place that is safe," he asserted. "They can see me through the cameras and hear me through the computers. There are cameras and computers everywhere."

I inhaled deeply and took the plunge. "What about the fifth floor?"

Scott's mother had been in the psych unit so often we had a shorthand term for it: the fifth floor. I explained the solution, trying to both stay with him and move him toward accepting help, adding, "They won't let anyone in who is not supposed to be there, and there are no cameras or computers in the patient's room. I think you would be safe there."

I knew immediately this volley had missed the mark. His face fell. "You think I'm crazy."

Now I had a tough decision to make. Despite his total departure from reality, he was smart and could read me. He knew what I was up to and would know if I were lying to him. I am a bad liar. I don't try it often because it makes me nervous, and it is really obvious. Scott may have been psychotic, but his intellect was fully intact. I stood up and took his hand. I looked into his eyes and decided my only option was honesty.

"Yes, honey, I think that you are sick. I think your brain is telling you things that aren't true, and they are scary things, things that would flip anyone out. I think if you got some medicine and rest that you would stop feeling the way you do now, and that would be a relief. Don't you think that would be a relief?"

For just a moment, I saw a flicker of vulnerability as if he were working out whether he should heed my advice, but then the wildness came back, fully inhabiting his eyes.

"Come here," he hissed and clamped down hard on my hand. He pulled me through the front door and to the computer screen where the Craigslist haiku page was open. "Look," he said. "Look at what they wrote."

He read me a couple of haiku; the themes were nonthreatening. I recall one about a farmer and a pig. After reading them, he looked at me with triumph, as if surely I understood now.

"Scott, I don't get it. These seem like normal haiku to me."

It seemed as if my clinging to rationality and reason drove him further from it. He became frantic in his explanations of what the codes were, what it all meant.

This type of delusion is common in psychotic episodes. It is a delusion of reference, where something benign in the world—a song playing on the radio, a headline read at a newspaper stand—is proof of another narrative, usually complicated and menacing. It is in the family of paranoid delusion, a delusion that causes one to believe they are under threat.

From these haikus he extrapolated that a group of women were monitoring him. He showed me random words strung together symbolizing a description of where he had been in the previous days. He pointed out sentences conveying a plan to hack our bank accounts. The one he was most upset by was a haiku which mentioned "a son." He was convinced they meant to harm our son.

I stood shocked and helpless as he explained all of this. I was aware of Hannah's presence when she entered the room from the doorway behind us, glad she was hearing this too. It was as if Scott were having a nightmare, yet I couldn't wake him. There was nothing I could do or say to help him be less afraid. The only thing that would help him now was medication: antipsychotics and mood stabilizers. I knew which ones, knew the names, but I had no access to those meds.

Over the next few hours Hannah and I sat with Scott, making multiple failed attempts at talking him into going to the hospital. He believed part of the gander stalkers' mission was to make him look crazy so no one would take him seriously. He was desperate for me to confirm his reality was true.

I kept thinking I should know how to handle this, being a mental health professional, having worked on the psych units and in a community mental health clinic. Here, now, in my kitchen, I was at a complete loss. I tried to walk the line between not validating his delusions as reality and trying not to alienate him. I asked more questions about the gander stalkers, about what he thought they wanted, what *he* thought we should do to help him?

In some ways his brain was a fascinating place to explore. I had always been interested in psychology, and this was the longest conversation I'd had with someone in full-blown psychosis. Yet the horror and helplessness were much more prominent than the curiosity, as it became clear I was not going to be able to convince him to go to the hospital. At some point past midnight I realized our children would be up in six hours or less and I had to get some sleep. I knew Scott wouldn't sleep, but I was also worried about Hannah downstairs on the futon. I knew that Scott needed some rest to help his brain slow down, but how could I get him to accept that?

I talked Scott into coming to bed with me. I was relieved when he agreed, though I knew he probably couldn't stay still long. We lay down together on our sides. I wrapped my arms around him and held him close, trying to convey that I was right there and I would do the best I could to keep him safe. Neither of us slept as we grappled with our own fear. After twenty to thirty minutes he silently got up. Finally alone, I let my feelings surface. I was reeling from all of the confessions Scott made on the porch. *He reached out to another woman? He was looking for sex with someone else? My God, what else did he do?* I felt sick to my stomach as I replayed his words in my mind. Yet, I didn't really have the space to deal with it. Not now. I needed to sleep and wake up the next day with a plan. These confessions would just have to sit alongside everything else I had put in the vault. Exhaustion overtook me and I drifted off, getting a few hours of sleep before my daughter was crawling in with me to snuggle and rouse me.

Chapter 9

I awoke the next day feeling surprisingly calm and determined. Hannah was still dozing on the futon downstairs with her daughter. Scott was sitting with our laptop computer, perched on a stool at the kitchen countertop. Mania can compel people to talk nonstop to anyone who will listen, and that's how Scott was when I headed downstairs from our bedroom in the morning. He immediately began to unleash a torrent of words as soon as I appeared. I told him I needed just a minute and went to get my youngest settled in for cartoons on the futon. I gently shook Hannah awake and we made a whispered agreement; she would hang close to the kids and keep them out of the kitchen. Soon enough, I was back to exactly the same spot I had been in the night before.

I sat at the kitchen table, drinking coffee and nodding as my husband rambled about gander stalking. I wasn't listening, instead silently crafting a plan to get Scott the help he needed. It was actually a game plan I had successfully executed numerous times when Scott's mother had become manic and I had needed to get her involuntary care. I knew who I needed to call, what I needed to say; in my mind it was simple. I just needed to get away from Scott long enough to make the phone call.

After about forty-five minutes of rambling, Scott stepped outside to smoke a cigarette and I took the opportunity to call the emergency services therapist at our local community mental health clinic and leave a message. I had worked at the same community mental health clinic for one year as a master of social work (MSW) student getting my clinical hours, so I was relieved when within two minutes I got a call back from a therapist with whom I'd worked in the past. I launched into a quick explanation of what was happening to my husband, with an eye on the walkway, aware I had only a few more minutes until he came back. In rapid fire clinical terminology I described his history of mood instability, paranoid delusions, sleeplessness, and nonstop movement. I asked the therapist to help me initiate an involuntary hold, as he was refusing to come in voluntarily.

The therapist immediately sounded wary. "Does he have a diagnosis of bipolar disorder?"

"No," I replied, "he was diagnosed with depression last year, but he wasn't totally honest when he went in, and he just went into a medical walk-in clinic. He was supposed to follow up with therapy and see a psychiatrist, but he never did."

"Has he threatened to harm himself or anyone else?"

"Well, no," I stumbled, "but he is so out of touch with reality, there is no telling what he might do."

"Look," she said in a tone I knew meant she was getting ready to tell me something I didn't want to hear. "I can't initiate a seventy-two-hour hold if he has no history of bipolar or psychosis, and he isn't making threats. He should go to the ER to be evaluated today, or you can bring him into the walk-in clinic tomorrow."

At this point I felt desperation overtake me. My voice pitched up as I said, "You don't understand. I have been trying all night and all morning to talk him into going to the hospital. He won't. He won't come in tomorrow either. He needs an involuntary hold. He is totally psychotic. There is no reasoning with him. Please, talk to the psychiatrist on call. He needs to be hospitalized."

I could tell the therapist was done with me when all I got was a curt, "I'm sorry, there is nothing I can do," and then the sound of a dial tone.

I sat in the kitchen chair, staring at the phone in my hand, caught completely off guard by the failure of my plan. It hadn't occurred to me he wouldn't qualify for involuntary care. In our state one has to be a threat to self or others, or gravely disabled by their mental illness, to have an involuntary hold placed. Wouldn't a person who isn't attending to their basic biological needs, eating and sleeping, be considered gravely disabled by their mental illness? If Scott were to go into the world paranoid and irrational, he could easily have an accident, or get lost, or if triggered, lash out at someone whom he thought was trying to hurt him. It didn't feel to me as if he, or I, were safe.

I was in this mental swirl when Scott walked back into the house. Looking up at him, I had no idea what to do next. So I just sat with him, trying to be as calm and reassuring as possible. He was so fragile. He was deeply wounded by the idea that anyone would try to hurt him. He looked at me with a bewildered expression and said, "Why are they doing this to me?"

He was filled with shame over what he thought the answer was: he'd proven himself to be unfaithful, to be driven by his sexual impulses. He apologized, telling me he would understand if I left him. I constantly reassured him I wasn't going to leave; we would get through this.

Hannah left by midday. She needed to get back home and prepare for work the next day. She looked worried as she packed up. We said goodbye standing next to her car. "Call me anytime you need me," she said. "I love you,"

"I love you, too," I said. "Thanks for staying last night. I know this was hard." She gave me a long hug. As she pulled away tears came into my eyes. I was on my own. I went back into the house and stood in the living room for a moment. I looked at the kids, both still on their screens. They had way exceeded our normal two-hour limit for screen time, but I wasn't about to stop them. It was better they were distracted. I hadn't had a waking moment without Scott cornering me since our talk on the porch the night before. I knew at some point I was going to have to tell the kids what was going on, but not now. I couldn't tell them with Scott hovering over me. I would have to find time later, and I would have to find words. Scott saw me standing there from his post in the kitchen, just inside the doorway, and immediately began talking again. The sheer volume of words was beginning to feel suffocating. I noticed my son look up from his computer at his dad, and then reflexively look away, as if he were unnerved. *I have to tell them soon,* I thought once more as I rushed to Scott's side and invited him to sit at the table with me just outside of my son's sight.

Trying to hold space for Scott and care for the kids at the same time was tough. I would usher Scott into other parts of the house when I needed to sit the kids at the table for a meal, so they wouldn't hear his constant narrative of persecution. Then I would usher Scott back into the kitchen and the kids out into the living room, where I allowed them unlimited screen time. I turned the volume up on the TV, which triggered my son to turn the volume up on his computer, in hopes neither of them would hear any of our conversation. The kids had to have known something was wrong, but neither of them asked me about Scott.

After getting our family through the Monday of Labor Day weekend, I was able to send the kids off to school on Tuesday. I canceled my appointments with clients and stayed with Scott. We were physically close during this time. It was as if my touch were an anchor, and he clung to me. We held hands as we talked at the table; we sat side by side on the couch. He would lean his head on my shoulder; I would wrap my arm around him. In these moments of stillness I tried to get him to agree to seek help. He always refused.

I was able to sneak in a few hurried phone calls on Monday and Tuesday to my family, letting them know what was happening with Scott. On Tuesday my mom suggested she pick up the kids and take them for a couple days. She would also talk to them about what was happening while they were safely away from it and had some time to process. I was grateful they would be spared seeing their dad this way. I was sure he would be in the hospital soon, and then the kids could come home. I continued to clear my calendar, telling my clients I was having a family emergency.

We got through the days okay, but the nights were awful. He would get ramped up, fervent in his need to convince me of his narrative. He wouldn't let me sleep, repeatedly waking me with fresh evidence of his persecution. His paranoia and taut energy frightened me. He moved quickly, acted impulsively, and in the back of my mind I was constantly considering my own exit strategies and noting where the phones were in case things got really bad.

I kept trying to talk Scott into going to the hospital or our community mental health center's walk-in clinic, and I called every provider I could think of to try to convince someone to hospitalize him. His primary care nurse practitioner had suddenly left the practice a month before, and no one else in the practice felt comfortable filling out the paperwork for an involuntary hold because they'd never treated Scott.

On Thursday I finally got Scott to agree to get help, but he refused to go to the hospital or our local mental health outpatient clinic, so we went to the medical walk-in clinic near our home.

Scott couldn't sit still in the waiting room. He paced in front of me, five feet one direction, five feet the other direction, for an hour. Finally, we were called back to an examination room. A nurse asked what brought us in, and Scott replied, "I've been under some stress."

I sat there trying to figure out how to insert some vital pieces of information without saying the words, *My husband is psychotic.* Instead I said, "He hasn't slept in the past six days," and "He seems very upset by some of the thoughts he is having." I hoped the nurse might understand my coded language. I had the sense she did not. When the nurse practitioner assigned to treat Scott came in, he introduced himself as Frank, and he had a calm manner that seemed to put Scott at as much ease as was possible given his taut state of mind. Frank asked Scott what was going on, and Scott launched into a much less paranoid version of the story he had been telling me. He said to Frank, "I haven't been faithful to my wife, and the stress is killing me. I feel so guilty about it, I can't sleep, I can't eat, I can't think about anything else."

He looked like a man torn apart by guilt. I was astonished at how he could pivot to such a believable story when he had been outlandishly irrational for days at home. I felt my stomach sinking as I realized Frank was not catching on to what was actually happening, and I couldn't say outright what was going on without alienating Scott. I repeated what I had told the nurse, but Frank had latched onto this idea that Scott was simply overwrought with guilt. If Scott's story were true, then Frank would get a gold medal for how he handled it. He was compassionate, telling Scott that marriages can be saved, saying to him it looked like we had a solid foundation because I was right there supporting Scott in this moment.

As Frank gained Scott's trust, Scott did begin to talk in a rambling, manic manner that could have indicated something more was at play, but I doubted Frank had enough experience with psychiatric cases to recognize it. Scott began to allude to there being more consequences for his infidelity, but he always skirted the outright delusional beliefs he was holding. As I sat there my anxiety rose from my gut through my chest and into my limbs. This was not going well. When Frank wrapped up the examination and left the room, I knew I had to find a way to speak to him without Scott present. I waited about ninety seconds and then told Scott I needed to pee. I walked down the hallway to a private nook where the providers went to chart and order medication. I found Frank sitting in front of a computer there. Frank smiled at me (the man was so pleasant), and said, "Oh, hello, was there something else you needed?"

"Yes," I replied. "I need to tell you what is going on with my husband, and I need you to prescribe medication to help him." I let Frank know I was a licensed clinical social worker and had worked on a psychiatric unit, so he would understand that I knew what mania looked like. I explained in my best professional language that my husband was psychotic, had been psychotic for days, and I believed he was having a bipolar manic episode with psychosis. I described his history of mood instability, other times when he had exhibited manic symptoms, and his frequent bouts of depression.

I begged Frank to prescribe the appropriate meds to end this. I suggested the medication Seroquel to Frank. I knew from working on psych units that Seroquel was often prescribed to bring someone down from a manic episode. Frank refused. He said those meds needed to be prescribed by a psychiatrist. I told Frank my husband refused to see a psychiatrist, and meds were our only hope to stabilize him. Finally, Frank told me he would consult with another doctor and assured me that if the other doctor thought it was appropriate, then Frank would prescribe meds to help my husband. I felt as if I had successfully conveyed the situation and had been heard. I walked back to the exam room feeling as if Scott and I might wake from this nightmare after all.

What Frank ended up prescribing, however, was Vistaril, a strong antihistamine used to induce sleep that does absolutely nothing for someone in the throes of mania. I felt my stomach clench when I looked at the discharge paperwork they handed us and realized what had been prescribed. I fought back tears as Scott and I walked to the car, the weight of our situation pressing down on me. Scott cried as we pulled into the Kroger parking lot to pick up his useless medication. He told me he had never felt so scared. He just wanted the gander stalkers to stop, and he didn't know how to make them stop. He was vulnerable, and helpless. I just kept saying, "I am so sorry this has happened to you." I did not say, "We'll figure it out," or "We'll get some help." It was becoming clear we were totally on our own.

I brought my children back home this same evening. My mom needed to be at work early the next morning, and I really missed them. My mom and I spoke on the phone and decided together to try keeping them at home with me. I hoped the Vistaril would at least slow Scott down. He had taken some in the afternoon and actually napped for a few hours. The evening went as well as it could, all things considered. Scott kept to himself, and the kids didn't seem to notice the disaster unfolding around us in our little bungalow. I got them to sleep without incident and talked Scott into taking more Vistaril before he got wound up. We watched TV together on the couch and I went to bed. On my way up I asked him to please stay off the computer because every time he got on it, he became very upset. He agreed, and I prayed for a quiet night.

In the back of my mind I was calculating what all this meant for my health. All the friends I had made in the Lyme community struggled with relapses into illness. There were some key factors that could influence relapse: sleep, stress, and diet. While I maintained the Lyme diet I had been on since 2016, I had no control over my sleep or my stress. The thought of becoming disabled by illness again in the midst of this already nightmarish situation began to cross my mind. I would quickly bat it away. It was too scary to entertain. As I did every night, I went to bed with a sense of urgency around actually getting some rest.

Some hours later, the sound of Scott's footsteps on the stairs startled me awake, my heart racing in anticipation of another ugly night of paranoia. He was moving quickly, in a frantic manner informed by the speed at which his brain was whirring. In no time he was hovering over me. "Get up," he said in a full voice, despite our seven-year-old daughter sleeping just feet away. I turned my head to read the blue glowing numbers on the clock, 3:24.

"Scott, it is three o'clock in the morning," I whispered. "I need to sleep."

"I need to show you something. Get up," he insisted, louder, closer.

I played through the scenario of further refusing in my head. He would escalate; my children would awaken. I would then be dealing with a psychotic person and two scared kids who needed to go back to sleep.

"Okay," I said, quickly throwing my legs over the side of the bed and moving toward the stairs so he would stay quiet when he saw me acquiescing.

I made sure to stealthily grab my cell phone and hold it against my palm and thigh, should I need to call 911. He was right behind me on the stairs, too close. All my alarm bells were going off, but I stayed perfectly calm, thinking if I could stay calm, maybe I could calm him too, and then I could go back to bed. My heart sank as he led me to the computer where I could see the Craigslist haiku page open. As soon as he glanced at the screen his face contorted with malice.

"I know," he said.

"You know what?" I asked.

"I know you are behind all of it."

He addressed me with shock and anger in his voice. I stared at him with a mounting sense of helplessness. I knew immediately I was in an impossible situation. Delusions are like an impenetrable fortress of irrationality. I remember my abnormal psych professor saying to us undergrads, "You can't talk someone out of their delusion. Don't even try." At the same time, I wasn't about to go along with it and claim responsibility for torturing him.

"Scott, I didn't do anything with those women. I don't know what you are talking about." I had no idea what else to say. I knew my denial would agitate him, but I couldn't find any other words.

"I found your messages. They are right here. You told me to stay off so you could send them messages, but I found them, I know."

"Scott, I told you to stay off the computer because every time you get on you get very upset. I promise I didn't send any messages. See, look at the time that one was sent," I said, pointing to the time posted next to the haiku he was referencing. "I was asleep then."

I could see him working through this in his brain, and hope flickered in me for just a moment until a triumphant look spread across his face as he noticed the cell phone I held cupped against my thigh. "You had your phone up there."

"Yes, but I was asleep," I insisted, knowing I had already lost him.

His eyes fixed on the phone again. I knew he wanted to take the phone from me, probably to look for more "evidence," but I needed my phone. I had my escape route planned and the phone was a part of the plan. The bathroom was behind me. If he made a move to hurt me, I could run to the bathroom, lock myself in, and call for help. Looking at Scott, the steely expression on his face, I quickly calculated that it was time to execute my escape. It was as if he read my mind; the moment my shoulder began to pivot toward the bathroom, he lunged. He grabbed my arm with a force that made me take a sharp inhale.

All he seemed to be aware of was the phone in my hand. He grabbed for it, and I jerked it away. He then grabbed the wrist connected to the hand holding the phone, the wrist that had never been quite as strong after it was broken. *Christ, he is strong,* I thought to myself.

I held on tight to the phone, struggling against him, but it was no use. I was still recovering my strength after two years of illness, and he easily overpowered me, taking the phone out of my hand. He placed the phone in a line of cell phones and the landline, arranged by the computer. Looking at the assembled phones I realized he had amassed all of my tools for calling for help.

Now, an abject terror began to rise within as I acknowledged the truth: he had a plan for me. I wasn't going to be able to cool the fever of his delusions. He put his palm on my back and pushed me toward the computer screen. My hand still throbbed from our scuffle as I stumbled toward the laptop. I regained my balance and looked at the amateur haikus, yellow letters against a black screen. Scott ranted about cracking the code, about the meaning of each one, about *gander stalking* and his persecution.

Finally, he got to his main point. "I know you are poisoning me."

He had pieced together that Frank, the nurse practitioner we had seen earlier, was working for me and the gander stalkers, and Frank had given him poisoned tablets. His eyes were wild and hard when he said, "I know you talked to Frank. You were both gone for a long time. Too long. Don't lie. I know, so you don't need to lie."

I didn't know how to respond, so I just stayed quiet, knowing I was trapped. There was no right answer. I had talked to Frank. He was right. There was no way he would believe I had merely been trying to get him help. I noticed his medication placed in the careful arrangement of items. Clearly the Vistaril had not touched his mania.

Scott followed my gaze to the bottle and snatched it up, opening the lid and pouring three of the pills into his hand. "Take these," he said. "If they are not poison you can prove it to me and take them."

I stared at the three pills, considering my options. I could take them, and it might temporarily appease Scott, but while three Vistaril probably would not kill me, they would render me unconscious for eight to ten hours, and it was now nearly 4:00 a.m. and my children had school in just a few hours. If I were incapacitated by the meds, they would be alone with their psychotic dad.

"Scott, this is your medicine for sleep. It is not meant for me. It would not be good for me to take it."

He looked into my eyes, his gaze holding no love for me. "You *will* take it."

"No, Scott, I won't."

A look of fierce determination came over him and he grabbed my upper arm tightly, drawing me closer, then he forced his chest against mine, his feet toe to toe with me, and began pushing me back until I was pinned between his body and the kitchen sink behind me. "You will," he insisted. He squeezed my arm with such strength that I knew there would be a bruise there the next day.

I searched his eyes for a sliver of the man I knew. The man who had held my babies tenderly, who had cared for me so well in the first year of my illness; he was nowhere. He brought the hand with the three pills to my mouth, pressing the hard ovals into my lips. I gritted my teeth and pressed my lips together. My terror ignited a primal part of me. I began to fight against him, twisting and pushing with my arms and legs until we both lost our balance and fell to the floor. Because he was still gripping my arms when we fell, I had no way to reach out and soften my landing. My head made contact with the floor, bouncing when it hit. I felt dazed for a moment, and he quickly gained the upper hand again, pressing my shoulders into the floor, climbing on top of me so he could pin my arms down with his knees to free his hands. He began to force the medication into my mouth. He was rough with me, his movements quick and aggressive.

When he pushed the medicine against my lips again, they felt bruised already from his first attempt. The pain of his full weight pinning my arms was excruciating. I clenched my jaw and locked my teeth together as best I could to prevent those pills from entering my body. It felt like I was being crushed beneath him for an eternity, my teeth clenched so hard they began to form fine cracks. In actuality, it was probably no more than three or four minutes. Finally, his own mind distracted him with another thought about the haiku, another piece of the puzzle he needed to show me. He climbed off of me, got to his feet, and went back to the computer, completely absorbed in the cryptic code only he could break.

I lay there and took stock of the room. I didn't have long until his focus would shift back to me. His back was turned and my cell phone was the last phone in the string of phones on the counter. My first thought was I might be able to grab it before his attention shifted. I very quietly got up from the floor and crept toward him on tiptoes, silently. The moment I was in reach, I grabbed the phone and in one swift movement turned and began to sprint for the bathroom. I could hear Scott's footsteps behind me, but I didn't pause to look over my shoulder. I reached the bathroom and leapt through the open door. Even in my terror I thought not to slam it shut, so I wouldn't wake the kids, but shut it quickly and quietly instead.

As soon as I turned the lock, I could hear him reach the other side. I instinctively ran to the farthest point from the door and pressed my back to the wall, sliding to the floor, wide eyes fixed on the door. I wasted no time calling 911. I knew if he wanted to get in, he could. The door was flimsy. He could probably break it down with his bare hands. He was a carpenter by trade, so if he didn't go with brute force he could easily grab some tools and take the door off the hinges.

Fortunately, he walked away from the door just after the 911 line began to ring. It was answered after two rings by a woman with a very calm voice. She was matter of fact, but I could also hear the concern in her voice after I explained I was locked in a bathroom, my husband had just attacked me, and I was afraid for my life. She asked me if there were any weapons in the home. "Just kitchen knives," I responded.

She calmly told me she would send officers right away, and she would stay on the phone with me until they got there. She asked me if I knew where my husband was in the house, and I suddenly realized I could hear him, and he was talking to someone. I slowly crept to the door and put my ear to it, and I could hear my husband saying, "My wife is trying to kill me." He poured his story out in a rapid sweep of words about being stalked, harassed, and poisoned.

My jaw dropped as I listened. I whispered into the phone, "He is in the room just outside the bathroom. He is on the phone."

He must have heard my whisper. Suddenly he yelled through the door, "I called the domestic violence hotline because you're trying to poison me."

Then I heard him go back to the call, which didn't last long. I still don't know what the domestic violence advocate told Scott, but it probably wasn't what he wanted to hear. In this moment, where fear was so dominant, I was struck by the absurdity of us both calling for help because we both believed the other might kill us. I nearly laughed, the impulse interrupted by the voice of the 911 operator on the line, asking if I was still there, still okay?

"Yes," I whispered. *How is this my life?* passed through my mind.

When Scott got off the phone he came back to the door and began to pound on it and jiggle the handle. My heart dropped and I felt nauseous. I yelled out, "I called the police. You need to get away from the door. They will be here soon." I hoped he wouldn't keep trying to hurt me if he knew the police would be there any second.

Those words I uttered had unintended consequences. On hearing the police were coming, Scott fled.

Chapter 10

Two deputy officers from the sheriff's department arrived on the scene just minutes after Scott fled. I heard the loud knock on the door when they arrived from my post in the bathroom. Because I had not heard any movement outside the door for several minutes, I felt safe to leave the sanctuary of the bathroom. After I ushered them in, the officers looked around the house to find Scott, yet he was gone. I quickly detailed the night's events, my clinical background, my belief I was witnessing a psychotic episode, and my fear for Scott's safety. I was adamant that if they found him he needed to go to the hospital, not jail. One of the deputies wrote up a report, and the other told me he would go look for Scott. The report writer left, and the remaining deputy looked for him for about an hour and then gave up, telling me around 5:30 a.m. the search was off. I sat on the couch wide awake. I didn't know what I would do when he came back. Would he try to hurt me again? Should I let him in? Yet, my bigger fear was Scott not coming back to me. I was gripped with anxiety at the thought of Scott fleeing into the world, with no ability to reason, or care for himself. I worried he would get hurt out there and have no way to get help. Maybe he would die.

Then morning came. I got the kids up and ready for school. I packed lunches, brushed hair, kissed foreheads, and sent them off as if everything were okay, as if I weren't a wreck from all that had come in the hours before.

My mom took the day off work and came to sit with me. I told her about the night's events, and she told me I couldn't be alone with Scott anymore. We arranged for my dad to come over if, and when, Scott came back. We decided the kids would stay with my mom until we got Scott in the hospital. The only positive thing about my terrifying night was the kids slept through it.

Then my brother Sam offered to come and stay with us. My family was rallying around me, but I still had no clear plan. I called around about involuntary hospitalization again, explaining that Scott was now a danger to me because he had attacked me, but still got the same answers: I should bring him into the ER and call the police if I felt frightened. No one was going to hospitalize him.

When Scott hadn't returned home by midmorning, we formed a search party. His friends searched the woods near our home and drove out to spots meaningful to Scott. We all knew he took to the woods. It was his place of solace. I kept his sister in Montana informed. Worry wove a tight knot in my stomach. When the kids got home from school I tried to play at normality, but it was clear something was off. My mom helped get them packed for a longer stay, and then they left. As I hugged them goodbye, I was both glad to see them off to safety and sad I would be missing the creature comfort of holding them when I was feeling so frightened.

At 7:00 p.m. Scott walked through the door. He was ragged, dirty, exhausted. He explained he had run through the dark woods for hours, fearing for his life, until he found the other side of the forest, midday. Emerging near the campus of the large university in our town, he wandered for a while, feeling it was still unsafe to come home, until exhaustion forced him to surrender. He traversed a five-mile distance and then came back again at least as far on foot. He looked so weary. He had buried his cell phone, our son's cell phone, and his wallet in the woods because he thought he was being tracked.

I had devised a plan for when he returned. I would call the sheriff's department back out to do a wellness check and try again to get him hospitalized now that he finally met the criteria of "danger to others." He had tried to overdose me the night before; he could have killed me. When Scott went upstairs to lie down, I picked up the phone, already knowing in my gut this wouldn't work. Running through the woods all night had subdued Scott. He was as close to lucid as I had seen him since the night on the porch. I called anyway. I needed to feel as if there were actions to be taken, things to be done to end this. Sometimes we take futile actions in an effort to regain control, which generally speaking, doesn't work out very well. I decided not to tell Scott before the police arrived, just in case he decided to run again.

Within fifteen minutes, four deputies arrived. I was a little surprised to see so many, and then remembered the "take downs" I had witnessed or been part of on the psych unit. Ideally, you have a minimum of four people when you physically restrain someone. A person for each limb, so you can evenly distribute their weight and carry them to a bed—or in this case, a sheriff's car—after they have been subdued. This realization came as a relief. *They are anticipating taking him to the hospital,* I thought to myself.

I quickly went over my reason for calling, telling them about the events of the night before and ending my tale by asking for their help in getting him to a hospital. One of the deputies warned me they wouldn't be able to take him to the hospital unless they found evidence that he was a danger to himself or others. It seemed so obvious to me we had passed this threshold, I was a little shocked it wasn't a given. They knew he had tried to forcefully overdose me the night before and had run psychotic through the woods for hours; how was he not dangerous to me or himself? With a sense of resignation already building I led them upstairs.

The deputies filed into our hobbit-sized upper level. In another situation it would have been a comical sight. The ceiling was only seven feet tall, and the dormer holding our bed was a six-by-six-foot space. All these giant men were crammed into this area like sardines. Scott looked startled when four strangers walked in on him sleeping but seemed to quickly accept their presence.

I sat on one side of the bed, while the officers gathered at the foot of it. One of the deputies sat on the opposite edge, and after introducing himself, he began to ask Scott direct questions. Did he feel like hurting himself? No. Did he want to hurt someone else? No. Was he willing to go to the hospital right now to get help? Still, no. The other three looked as if they found this whole thing very awkward. Then the deputy talking to Scott shifted his tone, becoming more conversational, asking Scott what had happened out in the woods, what he had been thinking. Scott had an uncanny way of covering his psychosis, even on his worst days, when interacting with people who might have hospitalized him. He said we had a fight and he went out for a walk and got lost. The deputy was gentle and kept the conversation going until he got Scott to the point where he was able to acknowledge he was worried about some things and might have overreacted.

Scott said he knew he probably did need some help, but he was too tired to go that night. He said he needed to sleep. The officer made one last effort, and I pitched in asking him to please go now, telling him how scared I was. He agreed to go the next day, but he was firm on not going right then. Understanding the cycles, how he would wear himself down and have a brief respite from the intensity of the mania before springing back into the volatile and irrational headspace, I knew he would not go the next day. I knew by then I would be the enemy again, and he would be unreachable. I also knew there wasn't a damn thing I could do about it.

I saw the deputies out without pleading my case again; I recognized it didn't matter. One of the deputies hung back. He looked worried, and sad. He told me there isn't a lot that they can do in cases like these, and he was sorry for what I was going through. I felt my eyes fill with tears. We were both helpless, he and I. Both players in a broken system. I blinked back my tears and thanked him for coming out and trying to help. He told me to call them back out at any time if I felt unsafe. I walked him to the door, and as it shut, I felt small and scared. I was out of options, again. I called my dad, who had already agreed to come over if Scott returned. My dad was a veteran of the psych units, particularly crisis care, where he spent years caring for people in the grips of psychosis. If there was anyone in my life suited to helping me watch over Scott, it was my dad. He told me he would come right away. Scott stayed in bed and fell asleep. I sat downstairs in the quiet house, staring into space, exhausted.

My dad arrived within forty-five minutes and he and I sat together. Conversation with my dad is quiet, with long pauses as he thinks about how to respond. It felt right that night, the silences. The drive to solve the problem of Scott's psychosis was draining out of me. I felt limp, defeated. It was nice to be able to sink into silence when my brain could come up with no more answers. My dad seemed to understand. Having him there made me feel safe. I was humbled by his willingness to join me in chaos in order to protect me. I went up to bed and lay next to Scott. Being near him, my body tensed with the memory of the night before. Paradoxically, I also felt relief to have him there. I knew he was safe. Somehow, between the waves of anxiety and relief, I managed to fall asleep. I slept lightly, still on guard, and at some point around 4:00 a.m., I heard Scott wake up and head downstairs. I felt bad about how my dad would be woken up, but also grateful he was down there.

The next morning Scott was still relatively lucid, and I talked to him about what had transpired, shared how scary it was for me. Somehow, I seemed to reach him. My dad hung out in the kitchen while Scott and I talked in the living room, sitting close together on the couch, holding hands, and he apologized for scaring me and agreed to go to the hospital. I let my dad know the plan. My dad went home to rest, telling me on his way out that if things went upside down again, I should call him. He would stay as many nights as I needed him to. I thanked my dad, and then I moved Scott out the door as quickly as possible, knowing the window to his rational mind could shut at any time.

Upon arriving at the emergency department of our local hospital, I gave the highlights of the last week to the receptionist, and we were quickly put in a room to wait. Scott was calm at first. He wanted to make small talk about the kids; things felt almost normal. Then two hours went by. Scott began to talk more, to look anxious. He was still pretty rational but starting to question what was going on. Then another hour passed, and another. Scott was frequently asking me what we were doing there, why it was taking so long, and I was watching his eyes, looking for wildness.

Finally, after five hours, a social worker came in to assess Scott. She was kind, calm, and easy to talk to. Scott was as candid with her as he had been with anyone yet, and I felt actually hopeful for the first time in days. She told us she wanted to consult with a psychiatrist, and she would come back and let us know what our options were.

On her way out she asked Scott if he would be willing to sign in voluntarily for a stay in the psych unit so they could help him get better, and I was shocked to hear him reply yes.

I was hit with a wave of exhaustion as I realized I might finally get to rest. It had been too risky to let myself feel how desperately tired I was when there was no end in sight. As I was sitting there across from Scott, savoring the idea of sleep, I saw his energy shift. His eyes widened, he looked at me and said, "They don't have windows."

I replied, "They have windows. I used to work up there. I am sure they have windows."

Then he said, "You can't leave when you want to."

Shit, this is the crux of it, I thought. *No, you can't leave. That's the point.* And he knew it.

"I'll feel trapped," he said.

I brought my chair close to Scott, looked into his eyes, and said, "I can't take care of you at home all alone anymore. What I need to help you get better is medicine, and I don't have it, and I can't get it. I am scared and tired, and I want to take care of you, but I can't. I need you to let them take care of you here so you can come home better."

Scott looked at me; I could tell he was conflicted, his paranoia rising, but also his concern for me and himself still present. When the social worker came back just minutes later and told us that the psychiatrist had authorized a voluntary admission, I silently prayed he still had enough of his rational mind left to sign the voluntary admission form. She handed him a clipboard with the paperwork, and he read through it. Even when totally stable, Scott was the type of person who would not sign something without thoroughly reading it. I watched his face darken as he read through a document detailing the terms of a psychiatric commitment. He was pondering the loss of his liberty. The prospect of confinement.

He sat quietly clutching the clipboard for what seemed a long while, and then said, "I can't do it tonight."

At this, I burst into tears. I knew he wouldn't budge; his stubbornness was a defining characteristic. After some emotional negotiations he agreed to go to an outpatient appointment the following day but would not consent to be hospitalized. Because he wasn't saying anything indicating that he was a danger to himself or others, they could not hold him against his will. His attack on me somehow didn't qualify him. I begged the attending nurse and social worker to ask the doctor in the ER if they could give Scott medication for his psychosis. A shot of Haldol, something that would take immediate effect? The nurse left and came back about fifteen minutes later saying the psychiatrist on call would not agree to it because Scott had not been formally assessed by a psychiatrist and diagnosed as psychotic. The social worker looked at me with great compassion as she told me there was nothing more they could do for him that night.

I left my body, sitting in that tiny emergency room cubicle. I went far away, on autopilot, numbly walking the corridor, driving downtown. I don't remember how we decided to go out to eat, or what the drive was like. I do remember climbing the small staircase into our favorite Indian restaurant, sitting across from Scott, ordering wine, ordering another, and staring at him. Something about the wine, the familiarity of the restaurant, and the warmth in Scott's eyes pulled me into the moment.

We began to smile at each other, talk about our kids, make jokes. He held my hand. We shared bites of our dishes with each other. We exclaimed over how good the food was. It was as if each of us knew this might be the last time we would be together, really together, for a while. Despite the fact we were both still endangered, and our lives would be chaos again in a matter of hours, we enjoyed our meal. Loving my smart, funny husband was still one of my truths, and it was the one I chose to occupy.

Chapter 11

I had called my dad from the hospital, and he stayed with us again that night. My brother Sam would arrive the following day. Scott slipped back onto the laptop shortly after we returned home, and I could tell his paranoia was ramping up again. I knew he wouldn't sleep. I didn't suggest he come to bed with me. Having my dad there, knowing he would intervene if Scott woke me up in the night, gave me a sense of safety. I was exhausted from all the nights I'd been up with Scott, and the wine at dinner intensified my fatigue, so I actually slept deeply for the first time in days. I don't imagine my poor dad got much sleep downstairs with Scott pacing through the house all night.

When I awoke it was obvious at first glance Scott had spun out into full-blown paranoia again. I couldn't keep him away from the computer, and although he was quietly paranoid, I knew this didn't bode well for the outpatient psych visit scheduled at 11:00 a.m. My dad stayed in a twenty-foot orbit once I was up—as if he wanted to be close enough to stop Scott if he tried to hurt me, but also giving us a little space.

Around 10:00 I mentioned to Scott that we should start getting ready for his doctor's appointment, and he immediately shut it down. His rationale was it didn't make any sense to go see a doctor when a doctor couldn't stop this group of women from tormenting him. "What would a doctor do?" he kept asking.

He had been online all night and seen what the gander stalkers were planning. He knew they wanted him to seem crazy—that way, no one would believe him—and he couldn't get anyone to help make it stop. A flare of total exasperation arose in me. My thoughts blared in my head: *How on earth can I explain to him that all I have been doing for the past week is trying to make it stop? That the only fucking way it's going to stop is for him to take some serious medicine? And the only way we can get him medicine is to go to this fucking appointment.* So yes, this torment would continue, and at this point it appeared endless. I had run out of tears, run out of patience, and I was just pissed. Yet I knew if Scott picked up on any anger from me it would feed the twisted narrative in his head.

My dad was planning to stay until my brother got in, so I decided to take a walk. Moving down our country road, my body felt heavy with the weight of my own helplessness. For days I had been ceaselessly working through the puzzle of what to do, what next, whom to call, which words to try. Now I knew nothing would work. I was defeated. The psychosis had won. It had taken my husband, and I had no idea if he was ever coming back to me.

It was the beginning of a grieving process that would haunt me for years.

My brother arrived and more days passed with Scott pacing and raving. With the realization there was no end point, this was just our life, I decided to bring my kids home. They had been away for days and I missed them. My daughter was only seven, and it felt like a long time for her not to see her parents. My mom was trying to manage her full-time job and take care of them. I had Sam there now; he could help with the kids, and leave with them, if Scott became loud or violent. I moved the sharp knives into a hiding spot in the back of the closet and prayed I was doing the right thing. I am still not sure if it was a good call. Our house was a scary place to be. All the adults on edge—Scott because of his delusions, Sam and I because we had no idea what Scott might do next.

When the kids returned, Scott went quiet. He was largely keeping his paranoia to himself, I think, because he felt Sam and I couldn't be trusted. There was a part of me, though, that hoped he still had some sense of care for our children and was trying not to frighten them. He kept his distance from me, eyeing me warily when I came too close. The days of him turning to me for comfort were gone.

A few days after Sam's arrival it seemed like Scott's mania might be abating. Scott was suddenly more communicative. He ate dinner with us. He agreed to take an antihistamine to try to get some sleep. When I went to bed Scott was lying quietly on the futon downstairs, possibly even asleep. I crept as close as I could without waking him and heard his slow rhythmic breath. I knew manic episodes could resolve on their own eventually. Mania is not a permanent state, and I thought maybe, just maybe, Scott was coming back to us. I went to bed more relaxed than I had been since leaving the emergency department.

I awoke early, factoring in time for coffee before I had to start getting my middle schooler ready for his 7:15 bus. I sleepily noted to myself that now it was Sam asleep on the futon. Scott was already up and moving as I stumbled toward the coffee pot. I am one of those people whose brain is simply not online before coffee. When I went back to my beloved coffee habit in 2016 after several months of remission from Lyme disease, Scott quipped that I had gone "to the dark side." He remained loyal to green tea. I can feel the shift into alertness about three-fourths of the way through my first cup. Until then, don't bother talking to me unless you are okay with a grunt in response. It was in this state that I did something incredibly stupid. Scott approached me and asked if he could borrow my car. We had hidden the keys to his truck early on to make sure that if he fled, he wouldn't get too far. He didn't have any transportation options.

Scott seemed lucid. I thought he had slept. He told me he had done some research on natural treatments for bipolar disorder and he wanted to go to the store and get some supplements. After fourteen years of marriage the man knew me well. I am big on supplements and believe in natural healing; it was the perfect ruse. So, still asleep on my feet, I padded over to the spot I had been hiding my keys and dropped them into his hand.

The instant I did, I knew I had just made a huge mistake. Scott's eyes darted to our laptop, and I noticed he'd unplugged it. He suddenly pivoted, grabbing the laptop, and began to run toward the door. I saw where this was going and since I was closer to the front door than he was, I shot toward it. A hope that Sam, who was asleep on the futon just ten feet away, would wake up and help me stop Scott flashed through my mind. I called his name as I was crossing the threshold, but not loudly enough; he slept through it. Scott came charging after me, the laptop clutched to his chest. I reached the car first, planting myself in front of the driver-side door in a wide-legged stance, determined not to let Scott drive away. As soon as Scott caught up with me, I asked him, "Why would you need to take the laptop to the store?" The ice had come back into his voice as he said just one word, "Move."

I told him, "Scott, I can't let you take my car."

Scott repeated, "Move," louder and with more emphasis.

I said, "I changed my mind. Give me my keys back."

His voice lost the icy tone. It was full of fear and vulnerability as he pleaded with me, "You don't understand. Sam is in on it. He came here to help them. I saw their messages last night. They are planning to kill me today. Sam will let them in. He is in on it. I don't understand why you want me dead. You all want me dead. If you don't let me leave, they will kill me."

I stood there looking at him, knowing a paranoid man behind the wheel of a car was a recipe for someone getting hurt or killed. While keeping him safe at home wasn't going so well, there would be no way to keep him safe out there.

I took a deep breath to steady myself and said gently, "Scott, I am sorry, but I can't let you take my car. I don't think it is safe for you to drive when you are this scared. Please, just go back inside and we will figure something out. I love you. I just want to help."

At this he stiffened, his eyes hardening, "If you love me, you would let me leave. You're not letting me leave because you want me dead. I know. You are keeping me here because you know they're coming. Now, *move.*"

For a second I wondered if I should just get out of the way. I was getting nowhere with him. Then, an image of my car mangled on the highway crossed my mind, and I thought, *No, he could die. You can't let him go.* I resolved to be as stubborn as him this time.

With steel in my voice I said, "No, I am not moving. Give me my keys."

A determined look swept across his face and in one swift motion he put the laptop down on the walkway, swung his body back up, grabbed both of my arms forcefully and then tossed me to the ground like I was nothing to him. Just an object in the way. We had a gravel drive and I landed hard. Thankfully, my head and shoulders came to rest where the grass began. My thighs and calves, however, made contact with the hard rocks and I was stunned that he was capable of hurting me again, and how easily he had knocked me down, like I had no substance.

He grabbed the laptop, got in the car, and was already pulling away by the time I got to my feet. I stood dazed for a moment, watching my car receding into the distance as he drove. Dread flowed through my body, gripping my stomach. *He could die out there,* I thought once more.

I am not sure why my instinct was to keep calling the police. They hadn't been able to help us in any way thus far, yet the first thing I did when I went inside was to call the sheriff's department. I explained Scott had stolen my car and wasn't safe to be driving. I was worried for him and for others. The deputy I spoke with said the best they could do was file a missing persons report. If he was found somewhere there would be information about him in the system.

I agreed and within thirty minutes there was a deputy in my house again, sitting at my kitchen table, drinking coffee with me and asking questions. He started with, "What was Scott wearing?"

I replied, "A green and tan Patagonia shirt." *The one that brings out the green parts of his hazel eyes,* I added silently. "And a pair of tan corduroy pants." I thought about how those pants had become way too big for him over just ten days because he had eaten so little.

When we got to the question, "Has he harmed anyone or himself?" I glanced at my children, who were moving through the house getting ready for school.

The deputy instantly understood what my gaze conveyed and suggested we go outside. He hadn't been on any of the previous calls out to our home, and I knew I needed to tell him everything so he could help me build a case for hospitalization if Scott were found. He advised me, after I told him what happened, that I could press charges against Scott for assault. I sat with it, weighing the options. If he were arrested, it would get him off the street for a couple days. However, he wouldn't get treatment in jail; his erratic behavior could easily get him beaten by officers trying to subdue him; it would be more trauma for him; and ultimately, I would be the one paying the legal fees because it didn't look like he would be back to work anytime soon and I wasn't ready to leave him.

"No," I told the officer. "I just want him to get some help."

"Okay," he said, "let me know if you change your mind."

After the deputy left, I went back to my life, getting the kids on the bus, tidying the breakfast mess. Sam approached me, gave me a hug, and apologized for not waking up to help me. I told him I didn't think it would have made the situation any better. Scott was determined to leave, and we both might have gotten hurt had Sam woken up. I moved mechanically through the house, busying myself with tasks so I didn't have to think, or feel. After putting the milk away in the fridge, I noticed how bare the shelves were. I decided to go to the grocery store.

Dissociation is highly protective. As I readied myself and drove to the store I felt as if I were floating. I couldn't feel the pain in my bruised arms and legs. I wasn't focused on Scott, myself, or our children. Instead, I stood in front of the mirror numbly brushing my hair and teeth. Not feeling the bristles. Not noticing the dark circles under my eyes. It is not a good kind of floating, like the type that falling in love or achieving a dream gives you. It is a particularly cold type of floating, as if you are walking through a clammy fog. Pain and desperation are lurking somewhere, but all you can see is a thick wall of gray.

I drove Scott's truck to the store, relying on muscle memory, as my mind was a million miles away. Moving through the fluorescent-lit aisles I felt as if I were sleepwalking. The familiarity of grocery shopping was somehow soothing, but not enough to bring me back into my body. I was in the cereal aisle when my cell phone rang and a number with a strange area code appeared. I answered the phone after fishing it out of my purse, panicked I wouldn't get it in time, instinctively knowing it was about Scott. Upon answering, I heard a female voice on the other end. She asked if she was speaking to Scott Symanski's wife. She mispronounced his last name. "Yes," I stammered into the phone. She said she was calling from a hospital, one I'd never heard of.

My throat closed as I braced myself to hear the news Scott had been in an accident, but instead she said he'd been picked up by police and was in their psychiatric emergency unit. For an instant I felt jubilant, as I took this to mean the police had brought him in on a seventy-two-hour hold. Then the woman on the phone explained in a matter-of-fact tone that unless he signed a voluntary admission form, they would have to release him in two hours, since he wasn't saying he was going to hurt himself or anyone else. I sputtered into the phone all of my evidence for why he was a danger to himself and others, but the person on the other end was unimpressed. "Just come down here, and you can talk to the doctor about it." She gave me the name and address of the hospital, which I hurriedly scrawled on a crumpled receipt I had pulled from my purse.

Standing there, receipt in hand, I immediately took stock of my situation. I recognized the name of the town she gave me. I knew it was about ninety minutes away, so I had thirty minutes to get on the road. Then my phone rang again. This time it was a police officer from the small town where Scott was picked up. He told me Scott had come to a halt in the passing lane of one of the busiest three-lane highways in the Midwest, and he had fled the vehicle, run through the median for a couple miles, and then approached an outpost of the state police. He told me it was a miracle no one had hit the car when it stopped.

He said Scott was terrified when he approached the officer, insisting people were following him and trying to kill him. The police officer was able to somehow convince Scott he would be safe in the hospital, and that was how he came to be there. He told me my car was towed to an impound lot, and I would have to pay for the towing and a fee to get it out. I quickly clawed through the debris in my purse again, trying to find the pen I had just held as he gave me the name and phone number of the impound lot, which I added to a tiny blank space on the back of the receipt. Upon hanging up, I realized I would also need to take someone with me to pick up my car, and now I had about twenty minutes until I had to be on the road.

I wasn't sure how long it would take to achieve all of this, and someone had to be there when the kids arrived home on the bus. In my mind I designated Sam for that job. I knew he had to work remotely and I hated to ask him to miss more work due to my chaos. I frantically called my mom while standing in the grocery store, and she agreed to come with me. I raced home, abandoning the groceries. The next two hours were a blur of movement, dashing for my mom's green Honda the moment she pulled up, racing the clock down the same highway where Scott had abandoned my car. When we arrived at the unfamiliar hospital, I was directed to the psych wing of the emergency department, where I had to wait to be let in through the locked doors. I felt numb as I took in the shabby beige surroundings, everything a little dim and dingy. I was led to a small, padded room with its door standing open, and inside sat my husband, looking small, and scared, and unfamiliar in his hospital gown. He was sitting on a padded exam table of the same ubiquitous beige. I stood in the doorway, unsure whether it was safe to go into the room with Scott, not knowing how much paranoia this moment held.

Scott looked into my face, his eyes filling with tears. "Are you okay?" he asked, his voice hoarse and worried.

All the feelings I had kept at bay that morning as I was just trying to survive seemed to hit me at once, and my legs felt shaky. I moved to the one chair in the tiny room. Sitting so close my knees touched his shins, I looked up into his eyes and lied, "Yes, I'm okay."

We seemed to both have the instinct to grab onto each other, my hands moving up, his hands moving down, until they were intertwined. Tears began to fall from Scott's face into his lap. I could hear the gentle patter as they hit the thin cotton of his gown. "I am so sorry," he said, over and over.

"I know," I replied, grateful for the warmth of him so near, and for the paranoia's lapse so we could share just a minute together.

A nurse walked into the room and surprised me with the news that Scott had already signed a voluntary admission form, but he wanted to be hospitalized in our hometown. I was stunned, not able to believe he was actually going to get help. She explained they had already called the hospital in our town, and he would be a direct admit, bypassing the emergency department there. I would have to drive him, however, since they couldn't use their ambulance service for this type of transport.

Given that Scott's lucidity didn't have much lasting power, I was definitely concerned about traveling on one of the busiest highways in the state with Scott two feet away, but what else was I going to do? He was finally getting hospitalized, with just one more hurdle. He was given his clothes, and we were suddenly back in the world together, trying to make it to the hospital before the switch flipped again.

As we were buzzed out of the locked emergency unit, I remembered we still needed to pick up my car. My mom was sitting in the emergency room. She looked anxious when she saw Scott with me, thinking this meant he hadn't been admitted. I quickly explained that Scott would be admitted to our local hospital; I just had to get him there. Scott seemed uncomfortable with us talking about him and wandered a few feet away from us, his eyes on the ground.

"Can't they send him in an ambulance?" my mom whispered.

"No," I whispered back, "they told me I have to drive him." My mom looked worried. I changed the subject, saying we had better find the impound lot because we needed to get on the road. My mom agreed, and we all three loaded into her Honda. Scott sat in the back seat. I glanced at him in the rearview mirror. He looked pale, and tired. I noticed he had developed new wrinkles around his eyes and on his forehead. He looked like he had aged ten years in the past two weeks.

We were able to locate the impound lot quickly, and Scott stayed in the Honda with my mom while I paid a stiff fee to get my car back. Then we transferred Scott, and his plastic bag full of belongings, to my Toyota Prius. As I placed Scott's bag in the back seat, I noticed the laptop wasn't there. I peered into the hatch, and it wasn't there either. I climbed into the driver-side seat and looked at Scott, who was sitting in the front passenger seat. "Scott," I said cautiously, "do you know where the laptop is?"

Scott looked at me sheepishly. "Somewhere in Boone County. I threw it out the window."

My hands gripped the steering wheel a bit harder, and I made myself take a slow inhale and exhale. "Okay," I said, feeling a pang as I thought about all the pictures and videos of our children that were stored on our computer. Now forever lost. "We should go," I said, as I pulled out of the impound lot and followed Google's instructions to the highway. One eye on the road, and one eye on Scott. We were both quiet. The mood was grim.

I asked Scott to put on some music. He chose a Bright Eyes album, *I'm Wide Awake, It's Morning*. I let myself get absorbed in the music. Scott seemed to be deeply listening as well. The song "First Day of My Life" came on. Conor Oberst, in his trademark warble, sings about the realization that his lover is valuable—he wants to put the work in for the first time in his life. About a third of the way through the song Scott turned to me and told me whoever was controlling the radio wanted him to hear this song, because it was about him and me, about how he felt about me. He had tears in his eyes when he said he needed to remember how he felt about me. He told me he loved me and he knew I wasn't behind the plot after all. They wanted him to think that so he would lose me too, by pushing me away, but now he knew, and he would stop hurting me.

It was endearing, how his brain was trying so hard to give him a path back to me. I knew I couldn't trust it, not really, but I let myself sink into the song's lyrics anyway, imagining they were Scott's words to me.

The drive went smoothly, and Scott stayed calm as I pulled into the familiar parking garage attached to our local hospital. We held hands as we walked the path to the elevator. We stepped inside and I glanced at Scott as I pressed the button for the fifth floor. I felt sadness ripple through me as I remembered how Scott and I used to joke with each other when something in life seemed crazy, "Fifth floor, coming up," in reference to this very same fifth floor, where his mother used to spend time. While I had secretly harbored a fear that Scott's pattern of highs and lows were symptoms of bipolar disorder, I had always believed we would somehow circumvent him meeting his mother's fate. Neither of us ever imagined he would be here, in those smiling moments of, "Fifth floor coming up." I wondered if Scott was thinking about it too. I took his hand again and squeezed it.

We rose silently to the fifth floor, and I was grateful for the decisive way Scott strode toward the door to the stress care unit. A part of me still feared he might bolt. I picked up the tan phone hanging on the wall just to the left of the door. "Stress Care," answered a male voice.

"Hi, I am here with a direct admit," I replied.

"Name?" asked the voice.

"Scott Symanski," I answered.

I heard through the phone, "Okay, come on in," and then a loud mechanical buzzing I easily recognized as the door being released. I took one more look at Scott, smiled reassuringly, and said, "Okay," while pulling the door open before the window of release had passed.

When we stepped through the door into the unit, and the locked door swung behind us, I felt true relief for the first time since the moment we fell down this rabbit hole. Even with a voluntary admission, a patient can be held against their will on a locked unit while their physician reviews the case, should the patient decide they want to leave. If the patient is considered a danger to themselves or others, or the patient is gravely disabled by their mental health condition, the psychiatrist may ask a judge for a hold to continue treating the patient. Usually, the patient is granted release, but it takes twenty-four to forty-eight hours. Therefore, when the switch got flipped again, he would be safe and I would be safe, at least for a few days.

The hospital admission process was surprisingly easy, with just a few forms to sign. It was a little surreal to be walking my husband through an admission process I used to be on the other side of as a psych tech on this very same unit. I had sat in the same tiny intake room, and asked the same questions, taken the same set of vitals.

Scott looked scared when I left him, and I knew he didn't feel safe, but I couldn't stay any longer and so I turned and walked out of the bright fluorescent lighting of the unit. As soon as I heard the door click behind me a great weariness descended on me. I noticed the elevator was already on its way up, transporting someone else to the fifth floor. My eyes flooded with tears and I decided to take the stairs. I didn't want to see anyone else just then. I walked into the stairwell. It was quiet, familiar. A wave of grief rose within me, and I sat down on the top stair and allowed myself to weep silently. *How did we get here?* I asked myself. After a few minutes I wiped my eyes and nose on my sleeve and stood to leave. The realization I could offer my kids a safe home that night was comforting. *It will be okay,* I repeated to myself as I walked down the five flights of stairs and drove home to my children.

Chapter 12

The following days held some respite for me, but I was troubled by the haphazard care Scott seemed to be receiving on the psychiatric unit. Scott was not receiving therapy, just a very brief psychiatrist visit each day. I did not have the sense any of the clinicians on the unit had a handle on Scott's history, and when I pushed to be more included in his care, I was only given the opportunity to get a report over the phone from the nurse taking care of him. The "report" was just a med list and a reassurance that Scott was doing fine.

Scott's discharge was being planned by day four of his hospital stay. Scott's follow-up care was initially scheduled with our overburdened community mental health center. I had interned there as a grad student, and I knew properly caring for people was an impossible task given the sheer volume of patients assigned to each clinician. I lobbied for a smaller outpatient clinic to handle Scott's care and coordinated between the two, nagging the discharge planner for info needing to be faxed.

Scott came home in mid-September with a prescription for a strong mood stabilizer. He was also taking an antipsychotic which made him feel as if he were under water all the time. In the first few days we hung close together. Scott still needed the creature comfort of my warm soft body after a very scary two weeks, and I needed to see him go hours, and then days, without that paranoid look in his eyes. In some ways it was a sweet time, where we touched and hugged and talked.

I wanted Scott to take the rest of the semester off from his online program in environmental science. I had worked out a withdrawal arrangement from his classes with the college while he was psychotic, and I knew he could take time off without penalty. Scott seemed to understand this at first, but as the days wore on, he became desperate for normalcy. Diving back into school and construction work was how he thought he would accomplish this, so, as usual, he ignored me and worked it out to resume his full-time course load, and he also began to run his construction business again.

In the early days of beginning a medication, side effects can make functioning hard. The mood stabilizer he was prescribed takes four to six weeks to build to a therapeutic level, which meant it was extra important for him to minimize stress to prevent spiraling into mania before the medication had become effective. I was certain it was a bad idea for Scott to jump back into school and work at this moment.

The kids and I were in a tough position. Scott was undeniably sick, and the events of September 2017 were cataclysmic for our little family. Yet Scott had no interest in talking about any of it, and he became very uncomfortable when I attempted to acknowledge what we had been through. It seemed Scott wanted to pretend none of it had ever happened. I began to have conversations with the kids away from Scott, checking in to see how they were doing, if they had any questions. I found my children to be numb. They didn't want to talk about it either. I heard the message in their body language and their blank faces; they just weren't ready to face what had happened in our family. It seemed I was the only one who was. My son retreated further into video games; my daughter ate whole bags of Goldfish crackers; and I held the worry for everyone. Week after week I went to therapy, trying to work through everything so I could be strong enough to hold my family, and all of their unspoken pain, by myself.

The formal diagnosis of bipolar disorder helped me definitively put together a puzzle I had been working on for years. The pattern of the bipolar symptoms started with a very lovely phase of mild hypomania, where Scott was friendly, energetic, romantic, an involved parent, and a good friend. He happily worked on projects, brought me flowers, took the kids on outings, and was optimistic about our family and our future. Then he would move into mania: obsessive thinking about a threat, limited sleep, a lot of talk but no dialogue, and anger; lots of anger. Depression, the longest phase, came next. It could take months for Scott to emerge from the sadness and overwhelm.

Scott did okay through the rest of September. In the beginning of October he cycled into depression and his psychiatric nurse practitioner switched him to Latuda, a bipolar med that works better for depression. The med had side effects, including blurred vision. Scott couldn't do his schoolwork with his vision blurred, so he went off all meds after just a week on the Latuda and was waiting for his next visit to restart them. Luckily, he stayed relatively stable and was put back on Depakote in the third week of October. Scott seemed to feel better off the Latuda. He began to smile again, make jokes. It was nice to have him back after such a long time.

Months earlier, in June, I had signed up for an intensive training in a modality called eye movement desensitization and reprocessing (EMDR). The training dates were three days in mid-October, and three days in mid-December. I was passionate about my work and wanted a way to provide healing for my clients. There was a substantial amount of research heralding EMDR as the best treatment for post-traumatic stress disorder (PTSD) and trauma-related mental health challenges. EMDR uses bilateral (on both sides of the body) stimulation to open a client's neural network and allow them to process a traumatic memory in such a way that it reroutes the path the memory takes through the neural network. Once rerouted, a memory that had historically caused emotional and physical distress every time it surfaced, as if the trauma were in the present with the survivor, will become something that happened in the past. Something sad, and still not fun to think about, but not nearly as distressing. This rerouting affects so much, because it impacts the triggers for the traumatic memory, the memory itself, and also the associated memories, such as those that occurred around the same time. Essentially, EMDR allows us to actually change how our nervous system responds to our traumatic memories, which is life altering. Imagine living much of your life in fight or flight, and then finding the ability to have large stretches of calm, to be able to connect to others without sensing danger.

Although our situation still felt very tenuous, I wanted to attend this training. A high percentage of the clients I was seeing had a significant trauma history. I knew listening to them, supporting them, and giving them coping skills was helpful, but it wasn't enough to get to the root of their problems. I also knew from my own experience as a patient, EMDR was powerful. My therapist was using EMDR to help me process the events of early September, and the nearly psychedelic processing sessions allowed me to move through those scary memories with speed and grace, uncovering powerful messages of resilience, spoken from deep inside myself.

I left the kids with my mom and dad and drove the hour and a half to Cincinnati, Ohio. It was the first time since Scott's psychosis that I was alone for any length of time. I imagined I would revel in the quiet, but I found myself on edge, worrying about Scott home alone. The training itself was intense, consisting of hours spent packing dense information about the brain and its processing powers into my mind, and then practicing EMDR processing with others. I had just had a very traumatic experience, and EMDR brings up our trauma memories in a vivid and emotionally evocative manner. It was awkward sitting in a hotel hallway, sobbing hysterically while reliving the worst moments of my life. I talked with the instructor about it, but practicing EMDR, and experiencing EMDR, was a necessary part of the training, so I kept at it. Ultimately, it did help me feel more grounded. I went home relieved it was over, but also more in touch with myself than I had been since Labor Day. I reentered my life, grateful Scott had not become manic while I was gone. I focused heavily on my work, the one sphere of my life that felt in my control, and I jumped right in with EMDR. It immediately created positive results for my clients, and having something work well in my life felt good.

When Scott began to cycle into a hypomanic phase in early November, I didn't pick up on it. Scott was over the moon for me, so grateful I had stuck it out. He replaced the ruby in my engagement ring that had fallen out five years earlier. For years, every few months I would remind him it was still missing. I really wanted my ring restored. It was the only nice piece of jewelry I had ever owned. When he brought home the ring and presented it to me in November, it felt significant, like a new beginning. He looked at me with so much love in his eyes and constantly commented on my beauty and intelligence.

Looking back, I should have recognized this phase and known what was coming next, but I was in denial. After being rejected by Scott during his psychosis, it was incredible to feel so much love and appreciation from him. I leaned in. I stayed involved, making sure he was taking the medication, but

I didn't admit to myself, or to his psychiatric nurse practitioner, that I was seeing signs of hypomania. We rode this beautiful wave through Christmas and into New Year's Eve, where we celebrated in a hotel room on a family trip. We toasted the new year with sparkling cider, and I declared to Scott and the kids that 2018 would be *so much better* than 2017.

While the signs of hypomania could have tipped me off, I felt blindsided in January when I came home to find Scott in full-blown psychosis again. What made it even more alarming was the fact that I had gone back to leaving Scott alone with the children on Tuesday and Thursday evenings while I saw clients. When I walked into the house after working one Tuesday evening it was obvious Scott was psychotic and had been alone with our children for four hours. After two months of relative stability, I had really begun to think we had left this period of psychosis and dread behind us. It was if we had time-traveled back to those bleak days in September. The gander stalkers were back; I was enemy number one; and Scott feared for his life.

I quickly rearranged my life to accommodate his psychosis. This time, though, I accepted his psychosis as part of the fabric of our lives. I kept the kids at home and hired a babysitter for my evenings at the office, and I worked. Scott and I were both self-employed—no paid time off, no sick leave. We were just recovering financially from both of us not working throughout his first episode and my long period of unemployment during my illness. Also, my clients relied on me to support them. I didn't want to drop out of their lives again. It was odd, making arrangements with our college-aged babysitter, Maggie, knowing there would be a psychotic person in the house when she was there getting the kids off the bus. I carefully explained the situation to her and made sure she felt comfortable. I am not sure anyone could be entirely comfortable, but Maggie acted as if it were totally okay. She was a ray of light for my daughter, who instantly bonded with her. Maggie's upbeat way of being in the world was a good contrast to my overburdened energy. She took the kids on outings to give them a break from our sad, scary home. She never once appeared put off by our situation.

Every day I got up after a night of disrupted sleep, got the kids to school, and got myself to the office to begin holding sessions with my clients. It was a small miracle I didn't fall into a relapse of Lyme disease. The stress and exhaustion were crushing, but somehow my health stayed intact. I was careful to take my supplements, follow my diet, and hold onto my health. I knew if I went down again, we would be homeless in a matter of months.

One might question the ethics of conducting therapy while in a personal crisis; however, I was good at it. Becoming completely immersed in someone else's problems, experiencing their trust, and being able to offer comfort and solutions was a counterweight to the situation I was in at home. When I was with my clients, I was 100 percent focused on them. It was a respite. Our nervous systems travel through different states. Most of us are aware of fight or flight, but there are other places on the continuum. The loveliest area of the nervous system is the ventral vagal, the place of calm and connection. Because I had such a deep instinct to care for my clients, I would seamlessly enter the ventral vagal part of my nervous system at the start of each session so we could coregulate. In ventral vagal we are able to connect and feel safe. It was the only time in those winter months of 2018 when I was in a good spot in my nervous system. The moment I began to pack my office bag in preparation for returning home each day, an anvil of dread would lodge solidly in my gut, and I would move into a fight, flight, or freeze state.

I had my first panic attack driving home from my office one evening that January. I had to pull over, my heart pounding harder than it ever had in my life, a cold sweat breaking out all over my body, nausea and fear radiating up from my belly. Body-racking sobs escaped my throat as I sat behind the wheel. I couldn't sit there long, because Maggie would be bringing the kids home and I didn't want them to walk into a house populated solely by a mad man. Somehow I calmed myself, taking deep breaths, and repeating, "It's okay, it's okay," the rest of the way home.

Scott was experiencing something called rapid cycling. He would shift into paranoia and stay there anywhere from a few hours to a few days; then he would shift into a relatively lucid state of mind; and then into a crushing depression in which he couldn't get up from the bed or couch. Therefore, the first bout of paranoid delusions faded after just two days. After watching him cycle for about a week, he had a brief moment of stability, and in this lucid period between mania and depression he amazed me by willingly going to the hospital. It seemed like a miracle at the time to be spared weeks of psychosis, but because he was lucid upon admission, the hospital kept him for less than forty-eight hours.

When he was hospitalized, I found out that he had completely gone off his medication in early December. I had been asking him every day if he took his medication, but not insisting I watch him take it. He had lied to me nearly every day in December. Over and over, he lied. I reeled at his betrayal. The medication was the one thing holding our lives together. Without it his mental illness was a destructive force, pulling apart all we had built together over seventeen years.

I was completely unprepared for the short length of his hospitalization. He had gone in on the weekend, and I had planned to request a family meeting on Monday to discuss a more comprehensive strategy to help keep Scott stable. When I called on Monday morning to put my plan into action, I was told Scott was being discharged that day. When I protested, insisting I at least get a chance to talk to his psychiatrist first, the nurse I was speaking with flatly repeated he was being discharged because he didn't meet the criteria to be there and there was not going to be any meeting with the psychiatrist. So I went to the hospital, gathered up my very sick husband, settled him in at home, and prayed for safety and stability. He was discharged with a prescription for the same medication he had been on, Depakote, which took up to six weeks to reach therapeutic levels. When I read his discharge paperwork anger flashed through my chest. This treatment plan was thoughtless and futile. I knew there were many more options in modern psychiatry that could have been used to help Scott. They could have placed him on something fast acting, such as Seroquel, or they could have given him an injection of an antipsychotic that covers a patient for thirty days. Instead, they placed him on a medication that would require his compliance every day for weeks before it did anything for him. I steeled myself for the coming weeks, knowing he had not yet had enough days on Depakote to control his symptoms.

I was so beaten down at this point, I just felt I had to accept we were on our own. Scott had an outpatient nurse practitioner, but he wasn't able to reach Scott or compel him to stay on his medication. On his first day home Scott seemed to be okay. He was lucid and talking about some plans he had for getting back on track with work and college. I got the kids off to school and had one more conversation with Scott to make sure I was reading him correctly. It felt safe to leave him alone for the day, so I hugged him goodbye and went to work.

When I returned home to meet the kids' buses, Scott was gone. His truck was missing from the driveway, and there was no note explaining his absence. While I knew there could be many logical explanations for him going out in the world, I had a strong intuition that something was wrong. As I moved through my evening routine, I became increasingly worried. Scott missed dinner, and by 7:00. I was sure he had taken leave in a way more significant than running a mere errand.

We were in the last days of January, and it was bitterly cold. While Scott had not been psychotic when I left for work, I knew he could cycle into psychosis at any time. I called his sister, Sarah, in Montana, to tell her Scott had not been home when I returned from work, and I was very worried about him. She seemed to have the same reaction to Scott's absence; an immediate change in her tone indicated worry. She asked me to keep her posted, and to call as soon as he returned. As I tucked in the children, a fear began creeping into my heart more potent than anything I had yet experienced. Scott, when home and psychotic, was scary and unpleasant, but Scott out in the world in single-digit temps, paranoid and irrational, felt dangerous in a very different way.

He could die out there, my brain kept whispering to me, as I read bedtime stories, and kissed foreheads. *He could die out there*, it kept whispering, as I brushed my teeth, and lay awake in bed. While my husband had been transformed by this illness, and had his moments of rage in the past, I still loved him. I wasn't ready to lose him. So as the hours passed from evening to night, and night to morning, my desperation grew.

In the morning, I called the sheriff's department again to file another missing persons report. I also told the kids their dad was missing. My daughter was too young to truly understand and seemed to be okay, but my son looked frightened. I explained to him the police were helping us find his dad, and I hoped he would be back soon. My son asked me if I could come to his school and tell him if his dad returned during the school day. I told him of course I would, and I took him in my arms and hugged his stiff body. After he got on the bus, I sent an email to his teacher to let her know what was going on just in case my son seemed upset. Then, as I had been doing, I went to work. I sat with my clients, trying to push my own fear aside. I listened deeply, diving into their trauma as a way to get some space from my own.

Something deeply optimistic happens in the therapy room. Observing a person who has been hurt in unspeakable ways discover their voice, and watching them find the courage to go back into the nightmare moments of their past to pick up the wounded person they once were, to nurture that wounded part back to health, is the most moving and hopeful experience I have been given the opportunity to bear witness to. Moreso than birth, sex, or love, it is in resilience that I find profound, sacred energy.

In witnessing EMDR work, the human capacity for healing was irrevocably affirmed. I once worked with a sexual abuse survivor who imagined himself unzipping the suit of shame that had weighed him down since his abuse began at age nine, stepping out of it, and leaving it crumpled on the ground as he walked away. This same man was able to imagine the wounded child he once was. He imagined his child self lying on the floor, and his adult self going to the child, picking up his small body, and then comforting the child until he was at peace. Moments such as those stayed with me as I held on through the dark days of early February.

We can survive the most horrific things. Not only can we survive, we can thrive, with enough healing and support. I think my work saved me as I navigated Scott's disappearance. I felt as if I were being torn apart by the fear of Scott being dead, and yet, I knew from sitting with my courageous clients, you can be torn apart and survive. When the time is right, all those parts will still be there, and they can be stitched back together again. So I sat with my pieces, and I waited.

Scott was found, and then lost again, several times during his disappearance. The first time he made contact with the police was in a Verizon store in Denver, Colorado, on day three of his psychotic sojourn. Apparently, he had thrown his most recent cell phone away shortly after he left our house that January day, and now he wanted to call me. In his mind it made sense to go to a phone store to make a call. When the employees at Verizon had explained they didn't have a phone he could use just once, he got agitated and the police were called. The police discovered he was a missing person and called me while he was in their custody. I was in our bedroom folding laundry when the call came in. I noticed it was from an out-of-state area code, and I answered immediately with a breathless, "Hello?"

On the other end I heard a deep male voice with a hint of an accent that I didn't recognize: "Hello, is this Mrs. Symanski?"

"Yes," I said, "yes, it is." I somehow knew I was talking to a cop, even though he hadn't yet told me, and my heart began to race.

The officer continued, "I am with the Denver Police Department. We are here with your husband. It looks like you filed a missing persons report on him?"

"Yes. Yes, I did. Is he okay?" I asked.

"Well, he seems confused. We were called to a Verizon store because he was being disruptive. He said he wanted to call you."

"He *is* confused," I hurriedly jumped in. "He is confused because he is psychotic. He left our home three days ago and he has been out in the world totally psychotic. He has bipolar disorder and he is really sick right now. He can't take care of himself, and he shouldn't be driving. Can you take him to a hospital?"

The officer paused before answering, considering his words. "We can, if that is what he wants to do."

At this I took a deep breath, gathering the last shreds of patience I had left for this conversation. "Please," I said, "my husband is mentally ill. He is far away from home and is clearly a danger to himself because he cannot meet his most basic needs when he is like this. He doesn't eat, or sleep, and he is likely to kill himself behind the wheel. Or kill someone else if he crashes. Please, can you take him in on an involuntary hold? He won't agree to be hospitalized. He won't. We have been through this over and over again back here."

The officer's voice told me everything I needed to know with the first word out of his mouth: "Ma'am," he said more loudly and firmly than before, "he isn't saying he is going to hurt himself or anyone else. I can see that he is mentally ill, but that just isn't enough. I tell you what," he said, his voice softening a little, "if you can talk him into going to the hospital, we can drive him."

I knew the officer was trying to be helpful with this offer, but it felt like a punch in the gut. I wanted to yell into the phone that he had no idea what he was talking about, that he didn't understand, but instead I just sighed the word "Okay" into the phone.

I could hear the shuffling sounds of the officer moving through the space between where he was and where Scott was, and then the muffled voice of the officer explaining to Scott that he had me on the line, and Scott could talk to me now.

Suddenly, there was Scott's voice coming through the line, saying my name like it was a question, "Marabai?" The sound of his voice caused relief to ripple through me momentarily, until I remembered what I had been tasked with.

"Scott," I said, my voice coming out a bit squeaky through the tightness in my throat, "oh, Scott, I am so glad that you're okay." A torrent of words started to spill from me. I told Scott about how worried I had been, how I had no idea where he had gone, how the kids were frightened. I found myself repeating, "I didn't know where you were" frequently, as I tried to convey to Scott how much his disappearance had affected me. As if those words were somehow the key. At one point I was overcome with emotion and began to cry.

Into the pause my tears created I heard Scott say, "Well, aren't you a good actress." His tone was frigid. It was as if the ice in his voice traveled over space and time and injected itself into my veins. I felt myself going cold.

"Scott," I said, my throat tightening even more, my voice hoarse, "I don't know what you're talking about. Of course, I am really scared. You have been gone for days. I had no idea where you were, and you've been so sick—"

At that Scott interrupted me, "Just stop with your game. Do you think I don't see you? Do you think I don't know? You're a fucking sadist." He continued in a high-pitched, mocking impression of my voice, "Oh, Scott, I'm so scared. Scott, you're sick. Scott, I just want to help you." Then his voice dropped into a low growl, "I know you. I know what's going on. I was trying to call you to tell you that. I figured it out. You're trying to make me look crazy. You're trying to get me locked up." His voice began to rise: "*You're trying to kill me*, but I won't let you. I am going to get far away from you. You will never find me."

I held the phone to my ear in resigned silence, reflexively whispering into the receiver, "Scott, please . . .," knowing that nothing I said to Scott would break the spell. Then he handed the phone back to the officer, and in an instant, was gone again.

Days later I got another call from an officer in a small South Dakota town. She was much more kind and understanding than the Denver police had been. She said they were experiencing a snowstorm, and she had been called to a truck stop by an employee who said there was a man who seemed to be waiting out the storm. The employee reported the man was pacing and talking to himself, and he was making the staff uncomfortable. The officer told me she knew right away Scott was psychotic when she got there. She said she had spent a couple hours sitting with him in the truck stop, but she didn't have enough evidence that he was a harm to self or others to initiate an involuntary hold. She did, however, convince Scott to wait out the storm at a local shelter and had driven him there. She said she would go back in the morning and we could do a three-way call to make arrangements for Scott to get home safely. She talked to me for a long time that night; she was so reassuring.

After I got off the phone I found myself sobbing with relief, knowing he had been found and was safe. I had been watching the winter storms sweep through the Northwest. It was so good to hear that, for at least that night, I could go to bed knowing he wasn't lying dead in the cold.

In the morning the officer kept her word and called me from the shelter with Scott on the line. I appreciated her maternal stance with him. She was calm, and warm, but still, the situation was impossible. He was paranoid and unwilling to come home. She stated she had spoken with a local mental health professional and there was nothing anyone could do to hold him because he wasn't threatening himself or others. Scott did share that he was headed to his sister's house in Montana, and he planned to stay with her. It was a relief to know he had a plan that would put him somewhere safe. Ultimately, Scott insisted he keep going toward his sister, and there was really nothing to be done about it. With the click of the receiver, he was gone again, and this time into a South Dakota blizzard.

After South Dakota, I stopped sleeping or eating. I am not sure why his disappearance was my breaking point, but it simply undid me. I was clearly not okay. My mom asked my doctor to prescribe something to help me with anxiety, and I got a very small prescription for Xanax. I didn't take them while I worked, but I did when I returned home in the evening and when I went to bed, and they kept me sane enough to get through another day, and another.

A couple more days had gone by when I got a call from Billings, Montana. It was Scott this time, sounding more lucid than he had since he left. His voice sounded weary and thin through the phone.

When I heard it, I breathed his name, "Scott," as if I had been holding my breath for days. "Where are you?" I asked.

"In Billings," he replied. "I haven't slept much, so I had to stop. I was getting too tired."

"Good," I said. "Good, you need to rest. I am so glad you are getting some rest."

"I slept last night," he said, "but I am still tired. I just want to come home."

At that I paused. As much as I wanted him in my sight, to know he was here and safe, I did not want him back on the road. I knew from watching his cycles that periods of lucidity were often just twenty-four hours, sometimes less. He could easily cycle back into psychosis before he reached our home, with twenty-two hours of highway time between us. It was a journey that would take at least two days to complete, and we didn't have two days.

"Scott," I said, my voice as even and encouraging as I could make it, "I want you to be here with us too, but it is too long of a drive when you are already so exhausted. Your sister's house is just three hours away. Drive there today, rest, visit with her. You are so close."

There was silence for a moment as Scott took in my words, and then I heard him say, in a plaintive, almost childlike tone, "But I want to come home."

"I know, my love. I know you do," I replied, my energy shifting toward the maternal. "But it is too far. Please, Scott, just go to your sister's. You can be there by this afternoon. It will feel good to be able to settle in somewhere for a couple of days."

This time, Scott's response came much faster, and the vulnerability was replaced with defiance. "I am coming home." I could tell from his tone that the decision had been made. There would be no talking him out of it.

Despite knowing that it didn't make any difference, I said, "I think it is a bad idea. I don't think you're in any shape to make the drive. I wish you would change your mind."

"I'm coming home," Scott repeated. "I'm leaving now." Even when sane, Scott was incredibly stubborn, so yet again, he overrode my wisdom. This time, though, he called me frequently from the road and each lucid conversation made the hours in between bearable.

Then, on the day I was expecting him home he called from our favorite state park located just two hours away. I could hear the depression weighing him down on the phone. He said he could go no further. He had rented a room in the lodge there with a credit card he had been using to fund his travels and just needed to lie down until I could come get him. His voice, coming through the phone, sounded small and burdened. I canceled my appointments for the day, gathered one of his close friends, and we went to him.

I hadn't told Scott yet, but I decided I could not let him back in the house with the kids until he had been hospitalized again. I could see my son struggling with worry and sadness, and my daughter was showing signs she was absorbing everyone's anxiety. I couldn't let things go on like this. As much as I wanted to take care of my husband, I needed to protect my children. So on the drive home from the state park, as his friend drove Scott's truck, and Scott and I were alone together, I told Scott I was driving him straight to the hospital. He asked me if we could please go home; he just wanted to sleep in his own bed. He looked so frail, crushed by depression and shame for what he had done to our family, exhausted by lack of sleep and lack of food. I wanted to relent, but I held my ground, and he quit arguing with me.

When we arrived at the hospital Scott refused to go in. I knew I wouldn't be able to swing an involuntary hold, and I knew he would be psychotic again any minute. I couldn't take him home, and I told him so. I kept repeating to him he couldn't come home until he had been hospitalized and was stable. His friend had come to the hospital with us, and when it was clear we were at a total impasse he offered to allow Scott to stay with him.

Thus began another frantic period of trying and failing to get my husband help. When his psychiatric nurse practitioner refused to initiate involuntary treatment, I wrote to the clinical director of the mental health clinic in charge of my husband's care. In the email, after giving all the clinical information, I stated, "Some of the things he has done, such as drive delusional through a blizzard, I think constitute putting himself and others at risk. His paranoia toward me makes me feel unsafe. He did physically assault me when he was having these same delusions in September, and I don't see why it wouldn't happen again as he is stating the exact same delusions this time around. When not ill, he is a kind, gentle, and loving husband and father. This behavior is clearly the behavior of someone who is gravely mentally ill. I sincerely hope you can help get him hospitalized so that he can come back to himself and come back to our family."

It was all for naught, though. Everywhere I turned I was told Scott actually had to say, with words, that he was planning to hurt himself or someone else. Saying it with actions wasn't enough. Eventually, I caved. I could tell it was causing a strain for our friend to have Scott at his house. Our friend had kids as well, and it didn't seem right exposing them to a psychotic person in order to protect my own kids. So I let Scott back into our home. He promised me he would take his medication, and I monitored him taking it more closely than ever. For a tiny moment it seemed the meds might be working. Scott seemed more stable, began talking about the future again, and was happy to be reunited with our kids. He was affectionate and loving toward them, and expressed his gratitude at being let in. I was wary, but exhausted, and so ready to go back to a more normal existence. I let myself be lulled into a false sense of security. I remember leaving for work one morning without a whisper of anything being amiss with Scott. When I returned, the apple cart was already mid-turn.

Chapter 13

After getting the kids off the bus when I returned home from work, I noticed Scott was tense and quiet, not meeting my eyes. I suggested we all go for a walk together, since being out in nature usually soothed Scott's nerves. It was late February, but an unseasonably warm day. At first the walk was pleasant, normal, the kids chattering about their school day, telling us about the silly things their friends had done. My son was particularly into ducks, and always had some duck trivia he and his best friend had looked up. I relaxed a bit as we turned onto our neighbor's gravel drive, leading to one of our favorite trails. Scott had been totally silent the entire time until he suddenly asked, "What are we going to do about our marriage?"

I was bewildered by his question. In some ways it made sense—this year had been hard on our marriage—but it wasn't something I expected to discuss in front of our kids.

"Scott, why don't we talk about this later," I said in a calm voice, trying to stifle my own anxiety.

"No," he insisted, "I need to know now. How can I stay married to you after what you did?"

Oh no, I thought, *not this again*. I took a breath and said slowly, "I have told you many times, I didn't do anything to you. All I have done is try to get you help. Plus, we really need to stop talking about this in front of the kids."

Scott would have none of it. Instead he launched into a detailed explanation of all his paranoid fantasies about me in front of our children.

When I tried to walk them away from him, he followed closely behind, raising his voice. I had worked too hard to keep his paranoid delusions from the kids for him to be doing this now. For months, I had convinced Scott to follow me outside when he was beginning to give voice to his delusions while the kids were around. I had ushered them to bed when I saw him getting ramped up at night and had driven them to my mom's house countless times to protect them. And now, here we were. They were seeing it all and there was nothing I could do about it. I watched their energy shift from happy and excited to scared and quiet, looking at me with questioning eyes. I kept smiling at them, putting my hands on their shoulders, picking up the pace to as fast as my seven-year-old could manage.

Scott ended his diatribe by telling me he saw no way for us to stay married after all I had done, so he was divorcing me. I stopped short at this. I spun around to face Scott. In hindsight, it is astonishing that anything could still surprise me; however, this did. I looked at Scott wide-eyed, and then I looked at the kids' faces, which were just as shocked. After all these months of obsessing over how to heal Scott and how to keep our family going, carrying all the weight financially, doing all the childcare and the bill paying and the grocery shopping while coping with his illness, he wanted to leave me?

Some dam inside of me broke then; all the hurt and anger and confusion I had been pushing away came roiling to the top. In an authoritative voice I had only used once before with him, when I was preventing him from pushing our daughter to the ground the summer before, I said, "You need to leave. You need to leave right now."

It was Scott's turn to look stunned. Maybe he had expected I would beg him to stay, that I would give him my standard line, "We can fix this." But we couldn't—I couldn't—and I needed a break.

By this point in our walk, we were nearly back home. I stormed into the house and immediately called a close friend of Scott's who lived alone and had a spare room. This friend had helped me search for Scott months earlier and knew our struggles. I told his friend I needed a couple of days away from Scott and asked if Scott could stay with him. He immediately agreed. I went back outside and told Scott he needed to go to his friend's house now. He could come back in a couple days to talk things over, but at that moment I needed him gone.

Scott was calm; he seemed to agree this was the obvious thing to do. Maybe he felt like he needed some space from me, his tormentor? He quickly grabbed a few things and left me to explain to our children what had just happened. I told the kids Scott was really sick again, and when he was sick, he didn't know what was real and what was not. I told them the things they had just heard him say about me were not real. I let them know I didn't think he meant it when he said he wanted to get a divorce, and he was going to stay with our friend for a couple days. I reassured them that, when he was feeling better, their dad and I would work things out. My children were more upset than I had seen them yet. We were all getting to a place where our ability to cope was exhausted. I put on an episode of *America's Got Talent* and lay in between them on the futon in the living room, my arm around each of them, their heads on my chest, and let them both stay up past their bedtimes. None of us mentioned Scott again that evening.

The following morning, I got the kids on the bus for school, got myself ready, and stepped outside to leave for work. As I was approaching my car, I spotted Scott in the driveway loading up tools from the shed. He hadn't worked in nearly two months, so I suspected he wasn't taking tools to a construction site. I waved him down to find out what was going on. He told me he couldn't live here anymore after the way I had treated him. He was moving to Montana to start a new life.

You might think after the harrowing trip to Montana just a month prior I would have tried to convince him to stay, but I was so tired, I did not.

"Okay," I said, no anger left in me, just resignation. I turned and walked to my car, and without another word, I drove away from my husband and the life we shared. I drove to work and pretended my life was not falling to pieces as I held space for my clients. In hard times my mom loves repeating the line from Dory in *Finding Nemo*: "Just keep swimming." Drowning wasn't an option. I had too many people relying on me, so I just kept swimming.

After work I drove home and gathered the children off the bus. With dissociative calm I explained that their dad needed to take some time away and would stay with their aunt Sarah for a little while. My false serenity began to crack as I uncorked the bottle of wine I'd picked up on my way home from work. I began to drink as I cooked dinner, and without thinking about it I drank deeply. I am typically tipsy at two glasses of wine, and drunk at three. I was three glasses in by the time dinner was on the table. I fed the kids and settled them in front of the TV in the next room. When my mom came by after her twelve-hour shift ended, I was getting ready to pour the last of the bottle into my glass. My mom sat at the table and asked how I was doing. I had already told her the events of the morning on the phone.

Mid-pour, I began to laugh, an unhinged cackle that did not convey joy, but something much more complicated. I told my mom, "He wants a divorce. He wants to leave me." I launched into a tirade about the months and years I had spent dealing with Scott's instability. All the anger I had stuffed down deep inside of me sprung loose. I began to yell, oblivious to the kids overhearing. I didn't care. I was too mad to care, too drunk to care. I couldn't pretend any longer that I wasn't hurt. Whether Scott was in his right mind or not, he had just rejected me.

I was tired of not being seen by him. For years I had experienced invisibility as his anxiety, mania, and wounds from childhood prevented him from seeing me and my good intentions. I was over it. My mom was great. She listened until I was done. She saw the minute my anger eroded and the hurt underneath began to surface. She held out her arms to me, and I collapsed into her body as we sat in my wooden kitchen chairs, pulled close. I wept then, and it was a release of all I had held silently for so long. After my tears dried, I began to inhabit a different kind of calm, one that felt a little warmer than the dissociative version I was used to. I needed to let go. I needed to feel.

In the early days of March, Scott arrived in Montana with little drama or chaos. I appreciated the quiet of the house with him gone. I couldn't muster the energy to be afraid for him anymore, and with him gone I didn't have to be afraid for myself. I felt like I began to exhale after seven months of holding my breath. When Scott had proposed divorce the week before, I was hurt, but also did not truly believe divorce was his intention. His desire to divorce was based on delusional thinking. I figured he would call and apologize in his next moment of lucidity. I hadn't allowed myself to consider leaving him while he was sick and incapable of caring for himself, despite the danger he posed at times.

I heard from Scott's sister, who had been able to get Scott hospitalized when he transitioned into depression. She relayed a conversation from his intake at the hospital, in which he said he was depressed because he was getting a divorce. I realized he may be more serious about divorce than I had first recognized. I sat with it all day, asking myself again, did *I* want to divorce?

I had been in therapy throughout this entire period and had pondered this question at length. I had seriously considered divorce several times, most recently after our trip to the West Coast where Scott cycled from happy and excited to enraged and abusive. That trip was the first and only time Scott had laid a hand on one of the children. I was still considering divorce as an option the day I came home to find Scott psychotic, but the psychosis made me put the idea of divorce on the back burner. While the psychosis was terrifying, and some of the episodes left me with PTSD, I couldn't stop seeing Scott's fear and fragility. I felt as if abandoning him to his delusions without any support would be cruel.

But now the question resurfaced. Did I want to divorce Scott? This time the answer felt clearer. Yes. I did. If Scott was not going to be stable, which was looking more and more likely, then yes.

I was so worn down from living in fear for seven months. His absence from the house had brought me peace, and I never wanted to go back to the way things were. Not ever. Yet divorce still felt wrong to me due to Scott's vulnerability. Instead of telling Scott I was taking him up on the divorce proposal, I waited until he was out of the hospital and told him we needed to legally separate until he had stabilized. I told him if he consistently took his medication and attended individual therapy sessions, we might be able to save our marriage.

By the time Scott was out of the hospital in Montana, he was getting less enthusiastic about divorcing me, so he agreed to the separation. I went to a lawyer and got a legal separation started, writing out the terms and stipulations clearly.

My plan was that Scott would not return to our home until he had been attending therapy and taking his medication regularly. When Scott called me on March 25, just five days before our son's thirteenth birthday, begging me to allow him to come home and be with our son on his birthday, I relented. I told him he could stay with us temporarily, but he had to find his own place and he had to take his meds and attend therapy.

When Scott reentered our home, a great wariness descended on all of us. He was depressed, and I could see the strain on my children's faces as they watched their dad struggle. On April 4 the legal separation papers came in the mail. It felt like a sad punctuation to our already bleak situation. Scott attended a few therapy sessions and then began refusing to go. It quickly became obvious he wasn't taking his meds. I knew it was a matter of time before the depression turned back into mania. I couldn't do it again.

Daily, I told Scott he needed to leave. I offered to pay for a small apartment for a few months to get him out. I found places for him to move into with friends, but he wouldn't take any action to leave. It dawned on me that I would have to be the one to leave, as I couldn't force Scott off his own property. I silently grieved the loss of my home as I began to search the internet for a place where my children and I could live. I loved my little bungalow on 1.5 acres. I loved the soothing green of the painted wooden siding, and the colorful interior. I loved the trees lining the road, dogwoods and redbuds all lit up in spring. I loved the red fire bush that flamed in October. I loved the bathroom with the hand-painted Mexican tiles I had chosen myself and helped Scott install. Yet I knew leaving was a matter of survival. I knew one of these days Scott could seriously injure me, even kill me, if his delusions gripped him hard enough. I had to go.

By mid-April I had cobbled together a plan. I found an apartment I could move into on June 15, a rare find in a college town where all leases run from August to August. A friend who was leaving the country offered her home to us for three weeks starting at the beginning of May, and we could stay at my parents' house for the two weeks between my friend's return and our move-in date. Moving three times in six weeks wasn't ideal, but it was the best I could do.

In many ways I was on autopilot, going through the steps, not thinking about any of it too deeply; I was still swimming. The hardest part was telling the kids we were leaving the only home they had ever known, and initially we had to leave almost all of their belongings behind. I couldn't move those until June. Both kids balked at the idea, my son in particular. He didn't want to leave. He asked why it had to be us and not Scott who left. I tried to explain, but it was confusing and complicated.

Both kids were increasingly quiet and withdrawn as each day passed and we got closer to our move. Scott was too depressed to register much of a reaction when I explained to him a few days before we departed that we were leaving. He didn't meet my eyes when I told him. He spent the next few days lying on the couch staring at his phone, not talking, not eating. There was still a part of me that felt intense guilt leaving him while he was clearly crippled by his depression. I had offered to pay Scott's mortgage and bills through June to give him some time to get back to work. I was worried he wouldn't survive on his own.

However, I was beginning to understand I couldn't save him; I could only save my children and myself. During an EMDR session with my therapist I saw myself standing in the dark with Scott and the kids, and then handing Scott a piece of twine from a ball I held in my hands. I imagined myself, my son, and my daughter turning and walking away from Scott toward a light in the distance. The path the kids and I walked went from oppressive darkness to forested and full of light. With each step I released more twine to ensure Scott could follow us if he chose to. It got progressively lighter as we walked, the sunlight bathing the faces of my children, which had gone from grim to smiling. The ball of twine held tight in my hands.

Part III

Chapter 14

Just days before Mother's Day, the kids and I packed up some clothes, a few toys, and any essentials, and drove away from our home. I had hoped Scott would leave for a while, so he didn't have to see us packing up. He didn't. He stayed in the same spot on the couch, just ten feet away from the front door where he could see our every trip out to the car, carrying our things and, ultimately, our bodies out of this home. Scott lay with a blank expression on his face, staring at his phone, not acknowledging our leaving. I remember timidly approaching him after everything was packed, and saying something like, "Well, we're all packed, so we're gonna get going," and getting no response from him.

I wished I could tell him that walking out the home we had shared for fourteen years together was the hardest thing I'd ever had to do. That I felt something inside of myself break a little more with each box I carried out. That I loved him and wished for another way I could be safe. One that didn't involve leaving him. But I knew those words would not be able to penetrate his depression. I knew I would only hurt myself by being tender with someone who could not hear me or see me. So instead, I turned and walked away, taking care to close the door quietly on my way out.

Our first night in a foreign place felt awkward. I kept a smile pasted on my face, pointing out all the cool features of the large house we were staying in. It was a beautiful home, but we all felt lost in it. It wasn't ours. My son was away from his computer, which had been his place to escape to amidst all the chaos of the past year. He missed it badly. I missed my kitchen, the familiarity of it, knowing the location of each item. My daughter missed her playroom, where she had spent countless hours conducting elaborate narratives with her Playmobil queens and princesses.

We were displaced, and it was painful to watch my children wrestle with it. Plus, all of our routines were suddenly altered. I now had to drive both kids to their schools, located on opposite sides of town, then pick them up when I was used to having the bus pick them up and drop them at home. I had to rearrange my work schedule to accommodate this, plus just keep the mechanics of life going: grocery shopping, bill paying, cooking, cleaning. It felt wrong somehow, like life should just stop for a minute and let me catch my breath.

I have had several of my grief clients make the same observation. When you experience a major loss, it feels as if your life has come to a grinding halt, and it seems unjust that the world does not halt around you. It keeps going. Bills still need to be paid; your job still needs to be done. In some ways having tasks to focus on can be a blessed distraction, but there is always a part of you that thinks, *Can't I just have a minute?* No, the world answers, you can't.

I kept swimming through those first few days, but when my mom took the kids for an overnight on the third day after we'd left, I crumbled. I watched the kids walk out the door, then wandered around the empty house like a ghost, unable to settle anywhere. Finally I went up to the bedroom, full of someone else's things, and the enormity of my loss hit me. Suddenly I began to let out shrieking sobs that came on with such force I was knocked to the ground. My knees gave way, and I sank to the floor. I found myself face down on the bedroom carpet, sobs wracking my body, unable to do anything else but cry. I am not sure how long I lay there, but it felt like hours.

Every time I felt the sobs subsiding, another wave of grief washed over me, and they would begin anew. I was crying for Scott, for the way in which this illness had ravaged him, had made him foreign and dangerous, had taken him away from me. I cried for my children, for all they had seen and heard, for the way in which their sense of security had been stripped from them, for all of the pain their future would hold. I cried for myself, for all the moments I had been terrified, for all the impossible decisions I had to make, for the unbearable loss of my true love, my husband, whom I still held tight to in my heart.

I had never stopped loving Scott. Even as I began to know I couldn't live with him, my love endured, and now it felt as if holding this love just might destroy me. In Elizabeth Gilbert's book, *Eat, Pray, Love,* she talks about a similar moment. She describes sobbing on the bathroom floor, finally clear she was going to have to leave the life she had in search of a new one, the grief of that realization becoming all encompassing. I have often thought of the evening I spent on the bedroom floor as my "bathroom floor moment." For as I acknowledged my grief, I also acknowledged that I could never go back.

When the kids returned from my mom's, I did my best to pack away my grief. We began to create new routines, find new ways to cope. I spent time every evening with my daughter, her body tucked inside my arm, while we read *A Wrinkle in Time* before she went to bed. I hadn't read it myself as a kid and felt we might have been led to the book by some divine guidance when I realized it was about a girl who is searching for her missing father and grieving him. Then I would turn my attention to my son, getting one-on-one time with him after my daughter went to sleep. My son and I were much more connected during this time. Without his computer to escape into, he was more open to spending time with me. We sat on the couch together in the evening, watching TV, his head leaning into my chest. I was grateful for the comfort being close to him offered. I felt guilty for allowing him to drift so far from me in the past year.

As our time house-sitting drew to a close, I began preparations for a long-promised trip with my son. I was determined to pull it off. Years earlier, when we still had a future to look forward to, Scott and I had seen a documentary on PBS about coming of age. In it, the filmmakers had looked at the many cultural rituals around the world that celebrate a child's passage from childhood into adolescence, and toward adulthood. We were both struck by the importance of these rituals, and the lack of them in mainstream US culture. So, we talked with our then-eleven-year-old about what he might want in a coming-of-age ritual. It was decided a journey would be appropriate, travel which also involved what we jokingly referred to as "feats of strength."

We decided Scott would take our son on this journey. They would talk about what it is to be a man, as our son was taking his first steps toward manhood. We declared age thirteen the time to do it. Initially we considered the idea of Scott taking our son to Glacier National Park in Montana, to do a rugged, day-long hike between chalets. As my son's thirteenth birthday approached, it became clear Scott would not be able to do this, so my son and I made plans for me to take him. My mom agreed to take care of my daughter for two weeks so I could give my son this gift. I was grateful the stress of the previous months had not caused a relapse of Lyme disease and I was strong and healthy enough to accompany my son on this important venture. My son asked if instead of Montana, we could go to Florida. I think Montana had become sullied for both of us, and sunshine made a lot more sense.

The drive to Florida felt like throwing off a heavy weight that had sat on our shoulders for months. As we got further away from the Midwest, my boy and I became lighter. We took goofy pictures of ourselves with peaches at a roadside stand in Georgia and marveled at their delicious flesh. We got out and celebrated at the Florida state line, asking a stranger to snap a pic, smiling genuine smiles. I hired a fisherman to take us out to catch some snook, as fishing was my son's favorite activity at the time. Heatstroke and vomiting aside, he had a great time on the boat, and I cherish the picture I have of him holding a thirteen-inch snook, beaming with pride. We fished off the dock at Sanibel Island, explored the sites of Fort Myers, and then came the feat of strength!

On a steamy June day we drove into Everglades National Park, rented two bikes, and embarked on a fifteen-mile ride through alligator-infested territory. It felt just challenging enough to meet the criteria. It was glorious. We relished in the thrill of glimpsing an alligator just a few feet away in the shallows, but knowing the bikes were faster than the gators. We saw birds, turtles, and plants that were new to us. We were sweaty, exhausted, and triumphant as we pedaled over the fifteen-mile mark painted onto the asphalt, the numbers waving to us through the heat as we approached. I turned to watch my son's face as we crossed the finish line. I felt so proud of him. So proud for holding on to his joy through my illness, and his dad's illness. For still having it in him to seek out life, to join me in this moment, and be fully present in it. My love for him was palpable, moving through my body, bringing tears to my eyes. I hope he felt it.

We had only planned out the first part of our trip, the gulf side and the Everglades. Now, each day, we could choose our own adventure. We opened the Priceline app and perused our options, finding a room in Key West discounted 50 percent because the hotel hadn't yet filled it. We drove from the Everglades to Key West, both of us awed by the long stretch of turquoise on either side of the highway as we made our way into the Keys. We were hungry and tired after our bike ride. We ate, showered, and crashed, both of us content and looking forward to the next day.

The following morning we walked the length of Key West, taking in the Spanish Colonial and Mediterranean Revival houses, and the vibrant colors everywhere—bright walls and flowers, and around every turn the shocking blue of the ocean against the white sand. We ate fish in a nearly empty restaurant, away from the strip of bars where obnoxious tourists flocked.

Next stop, a luxury hotel offering a room at a quarter of its normal price because it hadn't yet been booked for the next day in Key Largo. The hotel was close to a state park where we could go snorkeling, and so my son and I got to see the Great Florida Reef and its many colorful fish up close. We ate dinner on the deck of a restaurant that stretched into the ocean, sitting atop a peninsula, and we watched dolphins play in the water. It was perfect.

Our last stop was St. Augustine, the oldest city in the US. Founded in 1565, its labyrinth-like streets are filled with history. I had seen it for the first time as a teenager. Being in St. Augustine is like stepping back in time, with a lot of commercial tourist trappings thrown into the mix. It's the closest to being in Europe I have ever felt inside of the US, even more so than New Orleans, and I had wanted to show this to my boy. We walked around the old part of the city, reading plaques and visiting the fort that juts into the sea. Then we got into the car to drive home, both of us wishing we could stay on vacation longer.

We returned with only a few days left before our move into a three-bedroom apartment not far from the little bungalow we'd left behind. I tried to keep my grief at bay by shopping for our new life. It was the first time I had ever soothed myself via retail therapy. I had always been frugal, and here I was spending my life's savings on dishes, and rugs, and furniture. There was something liberating about it. One of the ways in which Scott dealt with the chaos of his childhood was to be incredibly controlling of his immediate environment. I had to get Scott's approval on any item I bought for our house. He almost always nixed the purchases I proposed, instead picking something out himself or insisting we could do without. I was never asking for anything particularly indulgent; new towels when our current set had holes in them, the necessities. I remember once, we had decided collectively it was time to replace our silverware after twelve years of use. I was out getting things for the household and saw a silverware set on sale. I brought it home, happy to have solved the problem, only for Scott to tell me I had to take it back because he didn't like it. Now, the realization that I could choose whatever I liked for my home brought me to tears in our local Kohl's store, clutching a set of teal dish towels in my hand. It had been so long since I had real freedom—from Scott's tight control of the house, from his moods, from his demons.

I put off the worst task until last: going back to our bungalow to pack the things we wanted to take with us to our new apartment. I had decided to leave Scott all the furniture, most of the cookware, and all the household items, as I knew he did not have the mental capacity to shop for anything. However, I had left weeks earlier with only a few changes of clothes, and there were toys, books, and personal items I didn't want to leave behind.

The kids and I came over with piles of boxes and packed as Scott lay passive on the futon, not looking at us or talking to us as we scurried around him. We all packed in a focused, hurried way. I felt the kids wanted to get out of there just as badly as I did. The second day I let the kids stay with my mom and I faced it by myself. When I was done, there was a massive pile of boxes in the living room that I would come to pick up the following day. The pile made me feel a little sick as I imagined Scott having to look at it every time he walked through the living room.

Walking into our new apartment for the first time was a punch in the gut. In our bungalow every detail had been attended to in the cultivation of a certain aesthetic. The trim was beveled and stained to accent the flooring. The stretch of hardwood floor in the living room had been restored by hand when I was seven months pregnant with our son. The claw-foot tub, the farmhouse sink, rescued from houses Scott had renovated. Here I was in an '80s-era apartment, stained beige carpet throughout, full of cheap flimsy particle board and old plastic. My son and I were the first to see it. I had to rent it sight unseen to be able to get in when I did, and my son could see my disappointment as I walked through it for the first time.

I took a deep breath and sat against the dining room wall, next to the sliding glass door. I wrapped my arm around his shoulder as he sat next to me. Were I alone, I might have cried, or sulked, giving in to my own feelings of sadness about where life had placed me, but I wasn't alone. I turned my head to look into my son's face. I could see his apprehension about our new home. I wanted him to feel safe here, so I said to him, "I was a little disappointed at first, but now that I've seen the whole thing, I am getting excited." Then I began to dream with him of what the place could be. I pointed to the space in the light-filled living room where we could put his computer, how great our new furniture would look with the natural light, how we could hang art to make it not so drab. My son's features shifted; he began to smile. I reminded him this place had three bedrooms, which meant he could have a real, regular-size bedroom. I gestured to the spot right in front of us and said, "The dining room table will fit perfectly here. It will be lovely."

He looked at me and said, "Mom, I love the way you can take a bad thing and make it a good thing. I love that about you."

I smiled at him and thought, *We just might be okay.* We were far from okay yet, but looking at my son's earnest face, a small, fragile hope began to bloom inside me.

I couldn't rest until I had made my new space beautiful, or as beautiful as one can make a crappy apartment. I arranged and rearranged furniture. I created ambient lighting and fussed over the placement of dish towels and knickknacks. I created color schemes and went in search of affordable art to hang. This is how I found myself combing the aisles of a low-budget craft store that had never really been on my home decor radar before. The kind of store that sells Americana-themed plaques, proclaiming things like "Home of the free" on them. The kind of store that invites you to "Live, Laugh, and Love" through doormats, mugs, and plywood signs.

I saw myself more as an original artwork, bohemian gal, but I needed some robin's egg-hued paintings for my new living room, and I had fifty bucks in the budget, so here I was, my eight-year-old in tow. As I was sifting through the generic art I came across a tan piece of cheap textured wood that read, "Someday, everything will make perfect sense. For now, laugh at the confusion, smile through the tears, and keep reminding yourself that everything happens for a reason."

As I read the words on the sign my vision blurred with tears that kept coming, two small rivers forming on the sides of my face. I stood frozen, looking at the sign, weeping silently. My daughter was distracted by her own search for art. When she finally noticed me, it snapped me back to reality and I wiped my eyes and quickly chucked the sign into my cart. I had just become an inspirational sign convert. God help me.

Every day spent away from my old life brought more clarity around the topic of divorce. At first, when we were house-sitting and the split was fresh, I would go to the little bungalow frequently to see Scott. I would beseech him to seek treatment, offering to be the coordinator, the chauffeur, anything to get him there. He would refuse me with a blank stare; not engaging, seemingly unmoved by all of it. I began to go less frequently after Florida. In late June I discovered Scott had not even attended his last appointment with his psychiatric nurse practitioner, and I had already known he was off his meds for some time, and not in therapy.

It had been three months since I had drafted our legal separation agreement, and Scott had done none of what I needed him to do to help me feel safe in a marriage with him. Living with my kids in our little apartment had allowed optimism to creep back in. There was nothing menacing around the corner. I knew I had control of what happened there. Scott knew where we lived, but he wasn't showing up on my doorstep. It seemed he wanted to avoid me. I watched the kids relax, easing into this new life, and I didn't want to go back. I felt done with uncertainty after so much of it.

I went to my attorney and initiated divorce proceedings. Then I went to Scott and told him I couldn't stay married to him if he wasn't going to try and recover from bipolar disorder. Scott told me it was what he expected and said little more. I made an attempt at some kind of closure, telling him I would always love him, even if I couldn't be with him, and I hoped one day we could be friends. He let out a dry, sarcastic laugh, the same one I'd heard through the phone when he called me from Colorado. It all seemed pointless, this moment, trying one last time to be husband and wife. I knew he would never be free of these delusions, and he would never see me clearly again.

He was lost to me, and I was lost to him.

The decision to divorce kicked my grief into high gear. For several months I had to stop listening to any music other than reggae, because a song could send me reeling with grief. I remember Ray LaMontagne's "Shelter," coming on while I was cooking in the kitchen, with the lyrics, *Listen, when all of this around us falls over, I tell you what we're gonna do. You will shelter me, my love, and I will shelter you.* I had to turn off the stove and run upstairs to the bathroom, where I got into the shower so I could disguise my sobs with the sounds of the rushing water.

In our wedding vows I told Scott I would be his shelter in life's storms. I felt I had betrayed him, betrayed us, by leaving. It felt like an impossible situation. By being tethered to a drowning man my kids and I would drown too, but the horror of watching Scott drown all by himself was nearly too much. Those months held many tearful therapy sessions, where I tried to EMDR myself out of believing I hadn't done enough to save him: If I had only tried a little longer, maybe I could still have an intact family. Maybe he wouldn't be at the bottom of the ocean.

More so than the shock of Scott losing his mind, it was the utter failure of my love for him to save us that rattled me the most. Over the years I had developed a steadfast conviction in the power of love as the ultimate healing force. Not just romantic love but love in all of its forms. I brought this belief into my therapy practice, unabashedly loving my clients—never in a way that crossed any type of sexual boundary, but in a manner decidedly intimate and profound.

I puzzled over the failure of love one day, as I drove the winding country roads out to my parents' house to pick up the kids after they had stayed out there. I couldn't stop thinking about how love had failed me.

I recorded myself on the long drive, saying in a voice strong at first, and then breaking and ragged, "*It's still inconceivable to me that love couldn't fix it. I truly believed that if I doggedly loved Scott no matter what, at some point he would start to strive for healing. I can't tell you what all the points of connection were in my mind to flesh out that belief, only that I had this almost mystical faith in the power of love. I think it is built by our culture, our films, our novels. I think it is built by faith systems, but for those of us who love people suffering from mental illness and addiction, many of us come to a point where we have to recognize that our love simply isn't enough to save someone.*

"*That there isn't going to be a day when they wake up and say to themselves, 'This illness is hurting the people I love and I have to do something about it.' It doesn't work that way. As a mental health provider, one would think that I would know that, but in my own way I bought into that idea 100 percent. I was* raised in a community that prized empathy but didn't have many boundaries. In trying to create freedom from the shame and rigidity with which they were raised, my parents and their friends accepted all kinds of behavior without judgment. The conversations I would overhear growing up had a lot more to do with trying to understand why someone was doing something hurtful, rather than the feelings of the person being hurt. Any type of actions they could take to protect themselves were not discussed. So as things deteriorated, I dug my heels in more and more. I loved so stubbornly, and with such ferocity. I loved almost as if love is its own form of battle. I will not let you self-destruct because I love you. I kept reiterating in so many ways that I would be there. I wanted him to feel safe, and loved, and like he had a safety net.

"Yet day after day would go by, week after week, month after month, where I could see it wasn't registering for him. He couldn't see me standing there, my arms opened wide. In fact, his mental illness twisted me into a sinister figure, someone who was out to get him, plotting against him; accusing me of poisoning him, accusing me of being the mastermind behind this plot that was robbing him of his sanity and his safety. And still I stayed, still I dug my heels in, still I loved stubbornly. It took the fear getting to a place where I couldn't breathe under its weight to start tamping down the love I had for him. Those weeks where the fear won out was the beginning of realizing that love was not going to win. It could not in that environment. Love was going to lose, and fear was going to win."

At this point in the recording anger began to creep into my voice. "Just about every fucking motivational speech you can think of warns you not to take that road. Right? How many times have we heard, 'Don't let fear win'? But, friends, love wasn't doing me any favors. Maybe sometimes, in some places, fear does need to win. Maybe sometimes, fear becomes your friend when it's telling you that you are not safe, in a situation in which you are truly not safe. Maybe fear makes you physically ill to wake you up to that reality. I sure didn't want to let fear win. I sure tried every avenue at my disposal to keep loving, to not allow myself the realization love wasn't going to work, but eventually it was the only place I could land that allowed me to leave the fear behind. Love wasn't going to work. At least not with Scott, at least not in that house, at least not in such close proximity to the madness. In walking away, I held onto a sliver of hope love would win at some point in the future, maybe not with Scott, but somehow love would redeem itself. I'm not sure where I stand today."

At this point in the recording my voice began to break. *"I continue to be heartbroken and shattered. Sometimes grieving people talk about losing their faith in God, but I think for me it's losing my faith in love. Love let me down. Love was not the unmovable force of epic proportions I had hoped it would be."* I remember sitting with these thoughts, driving and crying, feeling as if the very foundations of my psyche were rumbling. Then, as I did over and over, I pulled myself together and walked into my parents' house to gather my children.

In addition to narrowing my musical selections, I could only tolerate one TV show, HGTV's *Fixer Upper*. Any love story sent me into a tailspin. Any depiction of a fraught relationship brought back bad memories. I couldn't take any of it. *Fixer Upper* became a lifeline. Chip and Joanna Gaines were the restorers of wrecked houses. They would walk into a house battered by years of neglect and they would see the inner beauty. They would lovingly restore the house. Those walls, once streaked with grime and tattered wallpaper, would become smooth again, bathed in soothing colors. The trash would be cleared out to reveal beautiful floors. The terrible, heavy things that had created ugliness in the house would be thrown out. There the house would be at the end of each episode, open and beautiful, repaired and strong again. It was only later I would come to realize those houses were a metaphor for my life. I needed to believe in restoration. Seeing something damaged beyond repair, then brought back to life, was crucial to surviving the destruction of my family. I am not sure why Chip and Joanna's happy marriage didn't trigger me. I think I was just very focused on those transformed homes.

As I began to make sense of my marriage, I also began to think more about my illness. After recovering in 2016, I began therapy. In addition to exploring the questions my marriage brought up, I did some intensive EMDR work to process my illness. Once I gained some peace, my instinct was to put my illness behind me and not look back. Though I still had daily reminders of it, following a special diet for Lyme disease and taking a handful of supplements each morning, the terror and vulnerability I experienced throughout those two years was in the past. I wanted to keep it there. As my sadness around my marriage ending turned to anger at the medical establishment that had refused to help my sick husband, however, I realized I was also angry about how I had been treated by the medical establishment. I recognized it as an abusive relationship in my life, rife with gaslighting. It made my blood boil to remember sitting in the neurologist's office as he patronized me by disregarding every factual thing I said about conversion disorder, insisting on his narrative when his evidence was a lack of answers.

I was furious when I reflected on all those months adrift in a health-care system where no one would validate my experience of a crippling illness, where to a person they all intimated it had something to do with how anxious I was. As if anxiety is not a totally rational response to your body failing you at age thirty-eight, out of the blue, and with no diagnosed cause. Then there was the diagnosis of conversion disorder, a disorder rooted in Freud's concept of hysteria, a disorder that Freud was turned onto by Jean-Martin Charcot, who blamed women's uteruses for causing wide ranging medical problems. In a 2017 article titled "The History of Hysteria" published in the McGill University's Office for Science and Society's weekly digest, Ada McVean writes, "In essence, Freud believed that women experienced hysteria because they were unable to reconcile the loss of their (metaphoric) penis. With this in mind, Freud described hysteria as 'characteristically feminine,' and recommended basically what every other man treating hysteria had through the years—get married and have sex. Previously this was done to allow for the ridding of sexual liquids, whereas now the idea was that a woman could regain her lost penis by marrying one, and potentially giving birth to one."

Later research has determined that the majority of the medical problems women described that led them to be diagnosed with hysteria can now be explained by diseases that were yet to be discovered at the time Freud was conducting his research.

I thought about Freud's hysteria, about how women have been disregarded and abused in our health-care system since its inception. I began reading articles about how women weren't even included in most of the major research the medical establishment used to create its fundamental understanding of the human body and disease processes. About women experiencing heart attacks, being misdiagnosed as having anxiety, and then sent home to die.

I thought about the many female clients who had disclosed similar stories of being dismissed and misdiagnosed. One shared that at age thirty-nine she had begun to experience hot flashes, mood swings, and anxiety after a year in which her menstrual periods were quite irregular. She had seen her mother and aunts go through menopause and she recognized her own symptoms as such. She went to her male OB-GYN with the question, "Am I in early menopause?" Her doctor dismissed the idea immediately but told her he thought she may have a mental health issue and referred her to a psychiatrist. The psychiatrist met with her briefly and then prescribed a benzodiazepine, Klonopin, as a daily medication. The medication sedated her to the point that she was unable to perform at her job and was placed on a medical leave. In response to her complaints about how sedating the Klonopin was, the psychiatrist placed her on a second drug, a selective serotonin reuptake inhibitor (SSRI), Wellbutrin, which she reacted poorly to, becoming even more disoriented and dysregulated. This client had always believed in following medical advice. She felt as if she should take medication exactly as it was prescribed. Therefore, she kept taking both pills each day, despite how they made her feel. She tried to go back to work and was fired.

In the meantime, a precancerous cyst and three nodules were discovered in her breast, and she had to have surgery to remove them. She was fired just weeks before the surgery and lost her health insurance. Delaying the surgery meant risking cancer, so she had the surgery while uninsured. After six months on the medication my client, who had no history of bipolar disorder, had a manic episode and went on a spending spree across three states. In the immediate wake of this uncharacteristic behavior, she took herself off the medication and realized the devastation these meds had caused. She ended up having to file for bankruptcy due to the surgery, and the manic episode. Off the meds she was stable, able to get another job, and resume her life. She also discovered that she had, in fact, gone into early menopause. It took her years to rebuild financially from the damage done to her by the OB-GYN's misdiagnosis.

Another client told me she began having significant joint pain and fatigue in her early twenties. She chalked it up to exercising too hard or overextending herself at work. After her first child was born her symptoms worsened. She said just picking up her baby and doing household chores caused her excruciating joint pain. She went to a doctor who told her she was just stressed, and to try to get some more rest. It didn't feel right, but she was a young mother who had many other things to think about, so she accepted it and tried to manage her pain with supplements and dietary changes. The pain and fatigue plagued her for another five years. Through the birth of her second child, and her experience as a working mom, she had to struggle with these symptoms. While in my care she decided to look into her health concerns again, because it didn't make sense to be feeling how she did at age thirty-one. I recommended a doctor I knew to be thorough and listen to the wisdom of her patients. My client was diagnosed with lupus. She had lived with a painful health condition through some very important years in the lives of her children, even after she sought help. Lupus is a treatable condition, but without a diagnosis, no treatment was available to her. I felt angry on her behalf as we talked through her feelings about being misdiagnosed, the impact it had on her life.

In 1973 my own grandmother died from a misdiagnosed heart attack at age forty-six. She sought help multiple times over a period of two weeks, as she was experiencing a series of milder heart attacks. She was diagnosed with a culmination of viruses and sent home, where she had a final, fatal heart attack. In the 1970s, most of the research on cardiac arrest had been conducted on men. The medical establishment's discounting of the female experience of cardiac arrest led her doctors to miss what was happening until it was too late. My mom was only nineteen when she lost her mother, my aunt just sixteen. How many women have lost their lives due to the sexism built into the foundation of Western medicine? How many have suffered unnecessarily with debilitating symptoms? How many have experienced financial setbacks because they were misdiagnosed?

In sorting through my concerns about the treatment of women in the health-care system, I wasn't discounting the role trauma plays in our bodies. For many of my clients, trauma work is an important piece of the puzzle in regaining physical well-being. Unresolved trauma undoubtedly causes stress on the body, which can be a factor in many illnesses. In the mid-1990s, the Adverse Childhood Experiences (ACE) Study, which looked at the health outcomes of people who had experiences of abuse and household dysfunction in childhood, made a definitive connection between trauma and health, a connection many practitioners have observed for years.

What occurred to me as I thought about my experience, and the experiences of so many of my female clients, was it's not an either/or situation. The paradigm in Western medicine of *you are either stressed or you are sick* isn't serving us. People who are experiencing physical health problems exacerbated by stress and trauma still deserve diagnosis and treatment. Symptoms should be managed. There should be some effort to help patients be well. In the case of my client with lupus, supportive mental health treatment as an adjunct to the treatment of her physical symptoms has given her greater relief. In her situation, when she received a both/and response, getting treatment for both trauma *and* her physical health issues, it gave her the support she needed to recover her well-being. Had it been just one or the other, she may have struggled unnecessarily.

I realized Scott may have been as damaged by sexism as I was. When Scott's mother became mentally ill, the doctors took her husband's word for it. Scott's father had zero experience with mental illness—he was a salesman—yet they involuntarily hospitalized her every single time he called for help. When Scott became psychotic, I was able to speak from a place of authority, as a master's level, licensed clinical social worker, whose degree was concentrated in mental health and addictions. I had worked in multiple mental health settings, had seen psychosis firsthand, but no one would take my word over his. It was as if I had no voice. All over again I was shouting into the void. I couldn't get anyone to help Scott, and he drowned. I realized how shockingly similar the two experiences were. I could gain access to the people who had the power to help, but somehow when I spoke, they couldn't or wouldn't hear me. I wondered how many other women experienced this powerlessness, around their own bodies, around the men in their life for whom they couldn't speak.

In contrast to my protracted and futile search for help in the medical system, the legal system moved fast. By August we had mediated a divorce settlement, where Scott got the house, and I got the kids. I was awarded full custody and full decision-making power over visitation. Mediation was less painful than I had anticipated in certain ways, but more so in others. I was worried Scott would want joint custody and I would have to fight to be awarded sole custody, but he didn't question the custody arrangement even once. When the mediator began to ask me specifics around Scott's mental health and I disclosed the events of the past year, it felt shocking and shameful to admit what I had lived through. My hands shook as I gave the mediator and my lawyer the details of Scott's two assaults on me, his erratic and frightening behavior. The mediator then suggested adding in language ensuring Scott would have to be receiving mental health treatment before being allowed unsupervised visitation. I didn't expect Scott to agree to it, but he did. He agreed to everything with one small financial tweak. My attorney had added a stipulation, if the house were to be sold in the future, that I would get 10 percent of the proceeds. This would have put us at an even 50/50 split of the assets. It was the one thing Scott asked to be removed, and it felt worthwhile to me. I was far more concerned with keeping the custody agreement intact. We were done in a couple of hours; our lives permanently severed.

We had been together for seventeen years when I left our little bungalow. I left the same month we were married, and our fifteen-year wedding anniversary passed while we were apart. The finality brought me to a new place of grief, as well as a new place of hope; the two states created a roller coaster of highs and lows. I missed Scott, but I didn't miss his illness. I missed our family as it was, but I didn't miss the powerlessness I felt as I watched myself and my kids being hurt. So I did my best to accept what I railed against in my mind and body. Scott was lost to me.

Chapter 15

After the divorce was finalized, Scott seemed to find a bit of stability. I heard from a friend that he was working again, and when I had to contact him about taking over the mortgage payments on the house per our settlement agreement, he seemed more talkative and willing to work with me.

Like two people on a seesaw, as Scott appeared to rise out of a depression, I began to sink into my own mental health crisis. Living with Scott's psychosis had caused me to have a severe case of PTSD. In October 2018 my symptoms began in earnest. If I came home to an empty house, I would become convinced there was someone in it, lying in wait to attack me, despite the locked door. I had never in my life been a fearful person. I had traveled solo through Mexico with no worries. I had never locked my door at night prior to leaving my bungalow. During these episodes of PTSD, the rational part of my brain would try to speak up: "*Marabai, the door was locked; there is no way someone could have gotten in.*"

Despite the presence of rational thought, the fear was overpowering. I would walk through the empty house with trembling hands, looking in the closets and under the furniture, sometimes having to check multiple times before sitting on the couch, often unable to calm myself. The dread rising in me would culminate in a panic attack, and I would cry, shake, and gasp for breath until it passed. I became notorious for my heightened startle response at my office. If a colleague entered the kitchen while I was running water for the kettle, I would jump when I heard their footsteps or caught them in my peripheral vision behind me, my whole body trembling, my breath ragged. I knew it was uncomfortable for them—it was uncomfortable for me too—but I couldn't seem to help it.

I went to therapy every week, engaging in countless, grueling EMDR sessions to work on the PTSD. While I was doing everything I could to make the symptoms go away, my body was dedicated to feeling all the terror now that I was safe to do so. Every day spent in fear stretched me further. I was so tired. At night, lying in my bed, I would have flashbacks to scenes from the previous year—Scott holding me down and pressing those pills against my lips, or the sound my head made when it hit the dirt in my front yard. It was like being there all over again, and I would cry and pray to the Universe to make it stop. Sleep was elusive.

My mom saw me struggling and offered to take the kids for overnights frequently. While I appreciated the opportunity to take care of myself, I quickly realized sitting home alone was not a good option for me. My brain was bad company. I tried to connect with my friends, but all of them had small children and couldn't get away in the evening very often. So, one weekend when the kids were with their grammy, I made an online dating profile, complete with poorly composed selfies. I figured I could spend my free evenings going on comical first dates. Since I was looking for distraction, rather than looking for love, I imagined dating as fodder for funny texts to friends. I chose an app in which the woman makes the first move. It made me feel safer, and I hoped to avoid unsolicited dick pics.

I looked at dating as a grand science experiment. I was the researcher, gathering data on the person sitting across from me. I am fascinated by people, and I thought I could bring this curiosity to save dating from being boring or frustrating. It did not even occur to me that I might meet someone with whom I would want a relationship. Truth be told, I was just relieved to be doing something other than watching *Fixer Upper* and crying.

After seventeen years in a monogamous relationship, my dating skills were a bit rusty. My previous experience of dating in my early twenties was wildly frustrating. I would meet someone, think we had connected, hang out with him over and over again, going on these gray-area dates (a day trip to a neighboring city, cooking dinner together), and then after six weeks I would work up the courage to tell him I wanted to officially date him, and he would reject me with some version of "I'm just not into you." Even though nearly twenty years had passed, I still saw myself as someone men wouldn't find interesting. Not because I thought there was something wrong with me. I knew I was great. It was more that I believed men just couldn't see me. Therefore, I was a little surprised when four or five different men on the dating app actually replied to my initial message.

Several seemed genuinely interested. So I began the maddening process of texting with all of them at once until the time was right to meet in person. As a therapist you would think I'd have a leg up on figuring out the rhythm of the text-to-date dance, which is largely set by insecurities and unmet needs. Really, though, it was confusing and time consuming. My first couple of attempts at "Can we just meet so I can case you out for real?" ended with evasiveness or rejection (admittedly, I had only waited three or four days). I had little patience for the constant texting. I had signed up for dating, not hours on the phone typing out messages to men I wasn't even sure I liked.

After only one week I was not so sure this was for me. Then I came across a profile of a very handsome man, Alex, who looked vaguely familiar. His profile included a picture of him standing next to Booker T. Jones, and he was beaming with this infectious joy. I swiped right feeling more excited than I had about anyone else on the app. Just minutes later my phone pinged and I saw we had matched. I sent him a message and he responded immediately. We quickly established that we were part of the same group of friends but had somehow never managed to talk to each other, even though we had been in the same room on numerous occasions. We easily fell into a fun, back-and-forth conversation. I would ask Alex questions about the little I knew about him, and he would give me direct answers (with other men, it was as if they hadn't actually read my message before responding), but what I liked most about talking with him was how he would always comment on what I shared about myself and ask me to tell him more.

Alex also seemed very honest. He told me within days he was in recovery from drug and alcohol addiction, and about the impact his chaotic use had had on his relationship with his family. He seemed genuinely supportive when I shared a little bit about my situation with Scott, and he wasn't put off by my status as a single mom. We had only been chatting for four days when I asked him to go on a date with me. He said yes!

Meanwhile, I was also chatting with another fellow, Gary, whom I had connected with in my first couple days on the app. I was trying to set up dates for the coming weekend when my mom would have the kids to avoid the inevitable panic attack on the couch scenario. Even though I already had a lunch date with Gary on Friday, I set up a dinner date with Alex, too.

I hadn't gone on a first date in over seventeen years, and here I was with two first dates in one day.

Thursday night, after putting my daughter to bed, I tried on nearly everything in my closet. I had a lot more self-confidence at forty-two than I'd had at twenty-two. I was almost exactly the same weight, but in a college town teeming with slender young women, I'd felt fat and unattractive at twenty-two. After years of working to dismantle the cultural toxicity around women's bodies, and having countless conversations with my cool female friends about our work to accept ourselves, I had fallen in love with my body. I loved my curves. I loved my juicy thighs. I was also clear my body was primarily for me, and whomever I chose to share it with was one lucky soul. Choosing an outfit was more fun than painful. I finally settled on something casual, a pair of teal pants and a purple top that brought out the green in my eyes, and I went to sleep feeling the pleasure of anticipation. It had been a long time since I had felt anything similar.

On my date with Gary, I was surprised by how calm I was. After all I had been through, sitting across the table from a stranger seemed like no big deal. We met for lunch at a great Turkish place (he had good taste in food), and we talked about his work, and my kids. He was clearly nervous, and I wanted to like him more than I did just to help him feel comfortable. The truth was, while there was nothing wrong with him, I felt no pull toward him. He was not bad looking; tall and lean, with a kind face. I simply wasn't attracted to him. As we walked outside at the end of the date, he asked me if I wanted to go on a second date and I was honest, saying no, I did not. I figured stringing him along would be worse than just telling the truth. He took it in stride, and I walked away realizing I wasn't in any way disappointed about not wanting a second date. It was just as I imagined dating would be. I learned some interesting tidbits about geology (he was a professor at our largest state college); I had a good meal; and I was distracted from my own troubled mind. It was a win in my book.

My meetup with Alex was scheduled at 7:00 p.m. I had wisely scheduled a pre-date get together with my good friend Annie, who had been with me in the ER as a nurse when I became paralyzed. I went to her place around

5:00 to drink a glass of wine and catch her up on the developments in my love life. Annie and I were the same age and had been close since we were twenty, both working as perennially hungover waitresses at a coffee shop/ breakfast joint known for attracting a bohemian crowd. Annie had seen me through it all: my marriage, the birth of my children, my illness, Scott's descent into madness. I could've saved myself a lot of trouble listening to Annie's advice on men earlier in life. She took me aside after my engagement to Scott, a concerned look on her face, and said, "Are you sure you want to do this?" At the time I was so wrapped up in the idea of a fairytale wedding that I didn't see her warning, even for a moment. Now, sitting in her living room, sipping a cold glass of Riesling, I told her about my two dates in one day setup. She laughed heartily. After telling her all about date #1, I started to tell her about my next date.

"Wait, you are going on a date with Alex?" she asked, her eyes wide.

"Yes. Is that a bad thing?" I responded, fearing she knew some small-town dirt on Alex, and I had been totally off about my feeling that he was a good guy.

"Not at all!" she cried. "Alex is one of the best men in this town! If I wasn't already married, I would want to date Alex."

Relief swept through me. Yes. I was going to go on a date with one of the best men in town. Her endorsement of Alex felt like a real win.

Annie told me Alex was a hugger, so when I walked into the Mexican restaurant and saw Alex stand up to greet me, I went straight in for a hug. I think I surprised him a bit, but he rolled with it. When we sat down, I studied his face. He was more handsome in real life than he had been in his pictures. His mom was born in Italy, and he looked Italian: dark hair, hazel eyes, prominent cheekbones. I have always had a thing for Italian men. I was swooning the entire time my best friend Hannah and I traversed Italy when I was twenty-three. Alex had a gentle way about him. His voice was deep and held kindness and humor.

He told me about his difficult path through academia, having attended Yale straight out of high school, making it to his senior year there and then leaving when the pressure became too much. He finished his degree at our state school here in town and then went for a PhD in Italian studies. He was from a long line of academics, including his grandfather, a well-known and widely read musicologist. Alex described falling into a chaotic relationship with drugs and alcohol that began to consume his life. It was impossible to keep up with the rigor of his academic work while also feeding the demands of his addiction, so he left his PhD program.

I was touched by his willingness to be vulnerable, to share the more difficult aspects of his life. He told me about getting sober six years prior to our meeting, and how it changed everything for him. He had rebuilt a good relationship with his family, and he enjoyed his job at a local soup kitchen that fed many people each day. He was a musician, playing bass in several bands. He had good friends and seemed to have a lot of gratitude for his life now.

I shared a bit about Scott and the last four years of my life. How it had been turned upside down by my illness in 2014, and we had somehow gotten through that dark time, only to have Scott descend into madness in 2017; and then the divorce. My story was surely a bummer, but he took it in stride, asking compassionate questions, making me feel safe to share the answers. At the end of our date I wanted to keep talking, so I invited him back to my apartment for tea and conversation. We sat far apart, on opposite ends of the couch, and fell easily into a long talk. At the end of it, as it became clear it was time for him to go, I took his hand in mine and said, "My life is a little chaotic, with kids and interruptions, but if you want to see me again, I would like to see you again."

Alex smiled at me and responded, "I definitely want to see you again, and your type of chaos isn't bad at all. I totally understand."

We exchanged real phone numbers so we could stop communicating through the app and I went up to bed, a warm feeling nestled in my chest. *He definitely wants to see me again.* When I awoke the next morning, I saw a text from Alex: "Thank you for a beautiful evening. I was grinning all the way home."

Thus began my love affair. Truth be told, I was in no shape to fall in love. I was still reeling from what came before. I had only been on my own for six months when I met Alex. I was managing this cavern of grief waiting to swallow me up whenever I was reminded of Scott. I was a frequent passenger on the runaway train of PTSD. Yet, there I was. Quickly, and irretrievably, falling in love.

Alex and I saw each other the very next day, and in every spare moment thereafter. Not only could we talk for hours, but his touch was electric. It brought me back into my body after months of escaping my skin in order to feel safe. Alex was a great cook, and we would take turns being chef and sous chef, making beautiful meals together. We would listen to old soul music, and sometimes I would insist he slow dance with me. We laughed, played, and made love every night we could. My days were punctuated by the thrill of receiving a text message from him. He was all in. I was too, even though a part of me was like, "Girl, you are crazy for diving into this right now." I didn't listen. It had been years since something in my life had felt this good.

I didn't hide anything from Alex. He checked the closets and undersides of the beds with me when my PTSD was bad. He held me as I had panic attacks. He listened as I continued to make sense of my marriage. He called me a "badass" after I finally shared all the details of Scott's psychosis, the violence, the hard choices I had to make.

I had blamed the verbal and physical abuse in my marriage on Scott's bipolar disorder and confined it in my memory to the period between 2015 and 2018. Yet, as I began to find safety and security in my new life, my brain decided to dump the truth on me in an onslaught of memories dating back to before we were married. When I closed my eyes at night I saw Scott screaming at the twenty-four-year-old me in a strip mall parking lot, because I had said no to him about something, people staring at us, me thinking, *Oh no, they're going to think I'm in an abusive relationship.* I remembered Scott's face contorted with rage, yelling at the twenty-five-year-old me because I had used the oven to cook something on a hot day. I remembered Scott controlling every purchase we made. Scott telling me how any conflict in our relationship was my fault; he wouldn't get so angry if I could just get it right. Scott, in the grips of the first depression I weathered with him, telling me he didn't want to have sex with me because I wasn't attractive. Not because he was depressed.

I was still in therapy in early 2019, and these revelations just kept coming. I remembered an evening from years before, me sitting with my girlfriends, explaining that in a relationship it is normal for someone to be dominant and the other partner to be passive, and Scott just had more of an opinion than I did on most things, so I accepted he would dominate me. I recalled the uncomfortable silence in the room after I stated this blatantly fucked-up truth about my marriage. I remembered the way Scott mistreated me during my second pregnancy and then my illness, when I was completely dependent on him. I realized my marriage had always been abusive.

This epiphany heightened the emotional roller coaster I had been riding for years. The highs with Alex were much higher, and the lows of realizing I had been the victim of domestic violence were quite low. Scott was only violent with me when he was psychotic; however, he had been heading toward violence by dominating me, criticizing me, and controlling me for years. I could see the pattern now. It played out slowly, but it was still a recognizable pattern of abusive behavior. I felt so much shame around it. I, of all people, should have recognized the signs. I was actually working for a domestic violence agency in the early days of my relationship with Scott. I should have gotten out immediately. I never should have married this man. I berated my younger self for the choices I had made. My guilt was especially keen when I thought about my children, and what I had put them through by not leaving earlier.

My therapist helped me soften my stance toward my younger self. She reminded me I was a product of my culture, and although I had been exposed to and had adopted feminism, there were many more messages I had absorbed growing up in the '80s and '90s reinforcing the idea that my value was dependent on my attractiveness to, and ability to please, men. In 1989 I was thirteen, just coming to terms with my changing body, and it was clear from every magazine cover and TV show that attractive = thin. In the early '90s the biggest supermodel was Kate Moss, a skeletal figure plastered on magazine covers everywhere. I was round. I wore a size 16 in high school. No one who looked like me was held up as beautiful or desirable. Every rom-com in the '80s made it clear that being the girl chosen by the male lead was the whole point. The unchosen girls did not matter. The chosen were always thin. One *Cosmopolitan* magazine from 1997 held these gems all on the same cover: "What makes a woman bedable? Men Let You In on the Surprising Things That Make Them Lust After You"; "The 7 Little Signs He Loves You When He's Too Chicken to Say It"; and "Big Butt Be Gone: The Fastest Way That Works."

In the midst of this onslaught of messaging intended to let me know my goal in life as a woman was to attract a man, I had that period in my early twenties of confusing and demoralizing experiences with dating, only validating the cultural rhetoric. I believed I would have to live in a different body to have anyone desire a true connection with me, and that belief diminished me. When Scott treated me as less than, it felt true. Accepting this behavior as part of my relationship was my way of making amends for not being the thin, pleasing woman I was supposed to be. As the author Sonya Renee Taylor illuminated for me, it was my apology for living in a body that didn't measure up. When I realized my twenty-three-year-old self truly believed Scott was my one shot at marriage and children, and she was lucky just to have finally attracted a man, I felt sad for her. Sad that she had devalued herself, sad that underneath her facade of feminism, she was quietly affirming all the destructive dogma around women's bodies her culture offered up. I grieved for my younger self, and for all she had been through.

One particularly intense EMDR session helped me cultivate self-compassion. I saw a vision of a woman and instinctively knew she was a version of myself. She was gaunt, weathered, wearing a tattered gray dress, showing streaks of grime on her skin, stumbling into the new home I had made in this new life. She represented my past, what had become of my spirit over those seventeen years. I felt a searing sadness when I gazed upon her, and an overpowering sense of compassion. I imagined there was a new version of me, the present-day me, to welcome her in. I went to her, wrapped my arms around her, and sank to the floor with her, cradling her ragged body in my arms. She transformed into a perfect, new infant, and I placed her in a bassinet, wrapping her in blankets, lovingly putting my hand over her tiny beating heart. Then Alex was suddenly beside me and we were caring for her together, and I knew she would be all right.

After this therapy session my healing began in earnest. With the support of Alex, my family, my friends, and my therapist, I began to pick up the wounded parts of myself, cradle them in my arms, and nurture them back to health. Slowly, the PTSD symptoms faded. The waves of grief came less frequently. I began to trust there might not be some terrible thing around the corner. Somehow, some way, it would all be okay.

Scott had maintained a level of stability throughout the fall and early winter after our divorce but, as I rose up through the spring and summer of 2019, our seesaw reemerged and Scott began to sink. I had allowed some evening visitation with the kids at Scott's house when he was doing well, but when he began to deteriorate, I moved visitation to my house.

Scott didn't show up. He left the kids' lives without explanation or even a goodbye. For a few months I kept reaching out, trying to facilitate a relationship between them. He wouldn't respond to my texts or calls. Finally, I quit trying. I had very little contact with Scott. I still worried about him, wondering if he was eating, wondering if he was safe. I occasionally dropped off groceries, always noticing the weight he had lost since the last time I saw him, and his sadness.

In August of 2020, I helped Scott sell the bungalow. He could no longer make the payments. The sale of the house netted him eighty thousand dollars. I was relieved he had something to live on now. One morning, about a week after the sale, I noticed his truck parked in a deserted parking lot of a movie theater, shut down due to the pandemic. I stopped to talk with him and found him brushing his teeth. Clearly, he was living out of his truck, despite having tens of thousands of dollars in the bank. I was thoroughly confused. When I asked him about it, he said he had been camping. He seemed uneasy and answered my questions evasively. I sensed his paranoia and could tell I was freaking him out. I left quickly, hoping he would find a place to land soon. In the following weeks I sent him a few text messages, asking for an update on where he ended up but got no response.

About a month after seeing him in the parking lot, his friends and family began to reach out. No one had heard from Scott, and he wasn't returning their calls. His sister and I made efforts to track him down, sending emails and texts, calling, googling his name. Months went by with no word from Scott. In this manner, Scott left our lives. Without a word, he was gone. Not telling a soul who knew him his whereabouts. Just gone.

My children grieved the loss of their father quietly, not knowing how to give voice to it. We talked about Scott as you would someone who has died. I thought to myself, *I don't wish he were dead, but it would be more straightforward if he had died.* We could have a funeral, grieve, and work toward acceptance. His voluntary disappearance felt much more confusing and complicated. I made a point of telling the kids over and over that their dad had left their lives because he was sick. It had nothing to do with his love for them. I reminded them of how much Scott loved them.

As I let go of the family I had created with Scott, I began to form a new one with Alex. We cohabitated. I enjoyed falling asleep in his arms every night. We shared looks of amusement over the dinner table as my daughter talked endlessly about the topic de jour. We met each other with a hug each morning; we watched TV holding hands at night. I had to battle my own fears frequently, to be present to this, but Alex made it possible with his calm nature and easy reassurance. He was patient with my squeamishness around marriage. My fears around being too attached. My constant vigilance. There was a part of me that believed one day Alex would descend into instability or madness, and it took courage to stay connected to him.

When my fears surfaced, Alex reminded me that I was a badass. Over time, I began to believe it too. I was strong enough to face my fear. To hold onto what I had worked for. I no longer had the feeling that I couldn't believe this was my life. I could believe it. It felt like a life designed by me. It held what was truly important: my kids, my work, my love, and my voice. My voice. It was not extinguished, but strengthened.

Epilogue

The past is unmovable. We can't undo it. There will be moments when we remember it, and we will grieve. I will always wonder about Scott. Is he alive? Is he okay? Will he resurface? When I look at the totality of what we lived through, the kids and me, I am struck by our collective resilience. We are survivors, the three of us. We didn't drown. We swam.

In some ways we are still swimming. My son's grief has caused him to fray over time. Once a straight-A student in an honor's program he is now struggling to finish high school. He has dealt with some deep episodes of depression. He has given voice to my own thoughts: "It would be easier if he were dead." I knew exactly what he meant. Even though it would be sad and hard to find out Scott were dead, it would be final. We could grieve and find closure. I am sorry he has to live with uncertainty around something so important. I hope he hears me when I say I am right here for him. I always have been and always will be here for him, and I love him beyond measure. Losing himself in his computer has shifted into him finding himself in the music he makes on his computer. He layers sounds on top of each other to make intricate rhythms that throb through our house. Rhythms that are informed by his hard-won understanding of complexity.

Scott's disappearance has heightened my daughter's need to know there are things she can rely on. My daughter has needed me to be consistent. I have tried my best to do this. She needs to know she can count on the cadence of her days to be steady. I see this. I send her to bed at the same time every night. Every Friday night is family movie night. Every Saturday morning, I have something planned for us to do together. She hasn't grieved yet, not like my son has. She says she doesn't really remember her dad. I see the echoes, though. She loses her shine when the topic of fathers comes up in a show she is watching, or in a conversation with friends. She is an incredible artist. Her art is dark. Her subjects are often disfigured—an eye gouged out or a stitch across the cheek. I think she is working it out the best she can, with the tools she has. I am optimistic for her, and for my son too.

Maybe I do still believe in the restorative power of love, as I am holding my children in its light. I pray my love is enough to guide them through the destroyed landscape of our past, and into a future that holds ease and peace. Every day I honor my commitment to be here for them. We will always contend with Scott's absence. I have made peace with it as best I can. I finally understand contending with his absence is less painful than contending with his presence. I still hope Scott will one day get the help he needs to recover, and he will be a father to our children again in some capacity. I hold hope for Scott gently. My days of clinging to hope are gone.

My body is forever imprinted by Lyme disease. I still sink into weeks of nausea, headache, and fatigue when my immune system is confronted with any invader. I work hard at keeping Lyme at bay. I am healthy more than I am unhealthy now. In health, I am vibrant, strong, and driven. I don't take my own capacity for granted. Not ever.

For now, what I hold tight to are my children, my health, my peace; this new life I have built for us. It is good.

Alex has been with us through all of it. All of us sinking into grief at times. All of us grappling with the past. He has held steady. He has been kind and patient. He has supported me in writing it down. Our months together turned into one year, and then two, and now three, and still he is right beside me.

I know I won't be as I was before my world turned upside down. I know there are jagged seams and fine cracks that will forever be etched onto me. I hope when these marks, left by fear and desperation, catch the light, I will remember my strength, my ability to find my way out of the darkness.

Sometimes when a client has sunk into utter hopelessness, I will lean forward in my chair and cup my hands in front of me, and I will say softly, "I see you are without hope. Let me hold your hope for you. I will keep it safe until you are able to take it back from me and hold it for yourself." I can hold hope for myself now. I will never be able to honestly say I am glad for the fire I had to walk through to get here. However, it did transform my life into what it is today. I survived, and now I know that I can do anything.

I am glad for this life. Each day that is mundane and peaceful is a blessing. I will take all the blessings the Universe wants to give me. Thank you. Thank you. Thank you.

Acknowledgments

There are many people who have supported me as I have endeavored to write this book. First, I would like to thank my mom, Sharon Parsons, who has come to my aid time and time again, and whose love and support helped me swim through the hardest times. Mom, I love you beyond belief. To my dad, David Parsons, who helped keep me safe during the worst of it. To my kids, who were patient with me as I spent too many Sundays writing and editing this book. To my best friend, Clare Wildhack-Nolan, who always knows how to make me smile. To my brothers, Ben and Sam Parsons, who have supported me in ways big and small. To Alex, for sticking with me through the highs and lows, and for always believing that I could do it.

My biggest thank-you goes to Jim Poyser. Jim volunteered his time to edit the first three drafts of *Holding Hope*. Without him, this book would be a shadow of what it is now. I am still floored by his kindness and generosity. Jim, thank you isn't enough, but it's what I have to work with, so thank you, and I love you. I am not sure I could have begun this project without the safe cocoon of Women Writing for (a) Change. The encouragement I got throughout the writing of the first draft gave me the confidence to get to the finish line. I feel especially grateful for Karen Thursby, and Amy Beck, who saw me through the writing down of the darkest moments, and for Kelly Sage for holding the bigger circle around us. Thank you for resonating with, and honoring, my words. Finally, Alicia Ester and the team at Beaver's Pond

Press have been an invaluable resource, and I am so grateful I found my way to them.

There are so many of you who have supported me through your donations, your words of encouragement, and your excitement as I shared my progress. Thank you for all of it.

Made in United States
North Haven, CT
22 January 2023